WOMAN IN ANCIENT ISRAEL
UNDER THE TORAH AND TALMUD

with a translation and critical commentary on Genesis 1-3

by

Arthur Frederick Ide
Eastfield College

Mesquite

Ide House

1982

For further information on this or any other title
published by Ide House publishers, contact

Ide House, Inc.
4631 Harvey Drive
Mesquite, Texas 75150 U.S.A.
Telephone (214) 681-2552

Library of Congress Cataloging in Publication Data

Ide, Arthur Frederick.
　　Woman in ancient Israel under the Torah and Talmud.

　　(Woman in history, ISSN 0195-9743 ; 5B)
　　Genesis 1-3 in English, Greek, and Hebrew.
　　Revision of: Woman in Biblical Israel. 2nd ed.
Mesquite, Tex. : Ide House, 1982.
　　Bibliography: p.
　　Includes index.
　　1. Women in the Bible. 2. Bible. O.T. Genesis
I-III--Commentaries. I. Bible. O.T. Genesis I-III.
Polyglot. 1982. II. Title. III. Series.
HQ1132.I3 1982.　　305.4'2'0933　　82-9184
ISBN 0-86663-080-5 (lib. bdg.)　　AACR2
ISBN 0-86663-081-3 (pbk.)

Gratefully dedicated to

DELLA M. CHASE
Library of Congress

Whose professionalism, graciousness, and kindness has been without equal and of unsurpassed importance and value.

CHAPTER ONE

THE GENESIS OF WOMAN

The birth of a woman-child in ancient Israel was not a reason for rejoicing or celebration. A woman-child was a disappointment, for the father and the family had hoped and prayed for a man-child: a champion of the family who would toil beside the father and brothers, who would bear arms in defense of the land and hearth, and who would be able to carry on the lineage of the tribe. A woman-child was believed to be incapable of doing any of these things: at best her lot was to bear children, cook the meals, and keep the man's house clean.

According to the First Book of Moses, the woman-child was heiress to the lamentations and pains of Eve who was cursed by Jehovah to endure a multitude of sorrows including the sorrow of childbearing.[1] For that reason there was no special *berakhah* to welcome the woman-child into her new earthly home. In fact, generations later, under the Talmud, it was specifically ruled that there was to be no celebration of the birth of a woman-child.[2]

From the moment of her birth—until the day of her death—the woman-child/woman was considered to be less of a person than a man. She was considered inferior and unworthy of any significant attention—unless she was carrying that which could be a male-child under her breasts; it wasn't that she was considered a "second class" citizen—she was in truth no citizen at all for she was subject totally to the will of her husband, and her only responsibilities were domestic in nature and kind.[3]

Her subjection was graphically spelled out—even to her naming. for her introduction into the Israelite community as demonstrated by her name-giving was less important then the naming of a man-child. Even the choice of the name was secondary to the choice of a male name—and was subject totally to the discretion and will of the male head of the family who was never obligated to consult with the mother of the woman-child. He was the patriarch—the ultimate authority who represented Yahweh on earth.

The actual naming of the woman-child required the father to be "called to the Torah" (*aliyoh*) on the *Shabat* (or Monday, or Thursday when the Torah was read) immediately following the birth of the woman-child. Once the father was called to the Torah he had the option to invite his wife to accompany him. It was not considered essential for her to travel with him since, being a woman, she could not be called to the Torah which was exclusively a male responsibility and privilege. In most cases she stayed at home with the other young, beating grains into flour, watching over the flocks (and cattle if the family was well off), and tending to the fires. If she was fortunate she would hear of the incidents of the day in the evening hours.

When the father arrived "at the Torah" he read aloud the sacred writings. After the reading was completed he announced the child's name: taking it from the text of a special prayer (*mi sheberakh*), and asked Jehovah for health and blessings to come to the woman-child, while giving thanks to the Almighty that he was not born a woman—a thanksgiving which was to become a part of the Talmud:[4]

> *R. Judah says: Three blessings one must say daily: **Blessed (art thou), who did not make me a gentile; Blessed (art thou) who did not make me a woman; Blessed (art thou), who did not make me a boor.***

After the necessary prayers were said the woman-child was introduced to a wider circle of fellow co-religion-

ists, and from there to the circle of male kindred. Little did
the poor unsuspecting babe then know that this would be
her last chance at social intercourse with adult men prior to
her wedding and adult life.

But her infancy was not filled with a great deal of
sorrow. In fact she would know more happiness and pleasure while still an infant then she would when she grew and
"first discover her uncleanness": her first menstruation
which was damned as a mark of sinfulness and division of
the righteous from the almighty God. Pre-puberty days
were therefore special.

When the woman-child attained the age of puberty
her life changed as well. Her first menstruation was a cause
for weeping and wailing, and she would be sent away in
silence from the rest of the family for fear of contaminating
them with her uncleanness. So fearful was the family of being tainted by her menstrual blood that special dishes were
kept aside for her eating, as was a special bucket for water
from which she was to drink or use in her own hygene. So
terrified was the community as a whole of the menstrual
cycle of a woman that the Law was written damning any
man (or woman) to be near her: "If a man lies with a
woman having her sickness [the menstruation period], and
uncovers her nakedness, he has made naked her fountain,
and she has uncovered the fountain of her blood; both of
them shall be cut off from their people." Death or exile
was the punishment decreed for sexual relations during her
menstrual period in most cases, but occasionally the law
was relaxed to the point that "When a woman has a discharge of blood, which is the regular discharge from her
body, she shall be in her impurity for seven days, and whosoever touches her shall be unclean until the evening. ... And
if any man shall lie with her, and her impurity is upon him,
he shall be unclean seven days; and every bed on which he
lies will be unclean." The only way he could escape condemnation was to be shunned by all for seven days.[5]

Part of this great fear can be attributed to the fact
that the ancient Israelites considered blood to be the source

of life and thus the loss of any blood was the loss (or at the least the lessening) of life. It is for this reason that the men of Israel prohibited the eating or drinking of blood, ruling: "The life of every creature is the blood (*dam*) of it; therefore I have said to the people of Israel: You shall not eat the blood of any creature, for the life of every creature is its blood; whosoever shall eat it it (s/he) shall be cut off [from the community]."[6]

Exactly what was "blood" was unclear. Traditionally, and most cases state this to be so, blood was the "red fluid" that flowed in veins—however, the human semen (both male and female) was also considered "blood" and to let it flow without the possibility of procreation was tantamount to taking life—and at times, as in the case of Onan[7] could lead to the penalty of death (either divine or civil), but in most cases rendered the person who had released the "fluid" to be "unclean"—requiring a ritualistic purification: regardless if it was spontaneous emission, *coitus interruptus*, or masturbation. Its link to the menstrual flow was evident since the days of Moses who required the ceremonial washing of garments (and sexual abstinence), as well as the ritualist cleansing of anything else the woman or man touched.[8] It was especially true when (and if) she gave birth, for after the child had been born and cleansed of his/her mother's blood, the mother was ruled "unclean" as if she had menstruated: "*If a woman conceives, and bears a male child, then she shall be unclean for seven days: **as at the time of her menstruation**, she shall be unclean. And on the eighth day the flesh of his foreskin shall be circumcised. Then she shall continue for thirty-three days in the blood of her purifying; she shall not touch anything sacred, nor is she to come into the sanctuary until the days of her purification are over.*" Then comes the most sexist statement of all: "*But if she shall bear a female child, then she shall be unclean for two weeks, **as in her menstruation**; and she shall continue in the blood of her purification for sixty-six days.*"[9] Yet even here sexual discrimination did not stop. The woman-child's vagina would always be unclean because it was from the vagina that both the baby and the menstrual blood issued and rendered her unclean, while the penis was marked with favor by Jehovah through the ceremony of circumcision.

The woman-child had only one opportunity to make her presence in the temple: and that was rare. It came with her introduction into adult life—known as *Bat mizvah:* or becoming of an adult woman.

Bat mizvah permitted the woman to come to the temple on her own. And although the ceremony would develop over centuries, it remained still secondary to the male *bar mitzvah*, and it cost her her own participation in the community worship, while depriving her of all personal obligations of a religious nature of which only a few would be restored when she married an "acceptable" (*e.g.* faithful) Israelite male.

Bat mizvah was rare. It is customarily celebrated on Friday nights when the ark of the covenant is not opened and the Torah is not read. The ceremony has only adiaphoric trappings; even the special reading from the Prophets (*haftarah*) are qualified: for the ones that she would read that evening would be re-read in the morning after by a "qualified" (*e.g.* male) reader.[10]

After the ceremony the woman received meager tokens of compensation which have religious significance: she is allowed to inaugerate, participate in, and serve as celebrant in the lesser festivals of *milveh, kashrut, hallah*, and the lighting of candles.

Women had little opportunity to get around these restrictions (until just recently), for Israelite men saw women who claimed to have spiritual authority as demons, prophetesses, and sorceresses. In each case the assertive woman was viewed as being in league with the Devil. Such a union could only spell evil and destruction to the community. Therefore, to deal quickly and severely with it the law ruled with precise force that the woman was to be banned from the community or put to death, the latter being the penalty for prophetesses of false gods, and prostitutes (who frequently had the last laugh by marrying the very men who denounced them most vigorously, as was the celebrated case of the prophet Isaiah:[11]

וָאֶקְרַב אֶל־הַנְּבִיאָה וַתַּהַר וַתֵּלֶד בֵּן
וַיֹּאמֶר יְהֹוָה אֵלַי קְרָא שְׁמוֹ מַהֵר שָׁלָל
חָשׁ בַּז :

NOTES

1.   Genesis 3:16.

2.   *Berakhot* 59b, *Shulhan Arukh, Orah Hayyim* 223.

3.   Ibid.

4.   *Menahot* 43b.

5.   Leviticus 20:18; 15:19-20.

6.   Leviticus 17:14,

7.   Exodus 38:1-10.

8.   Exodus 19:14f; Leviticus 15:25-30.

9.   Leviticus 12:2-5.

10.   *Berakhot* 20b; *Megillah* 23a.

11.   Exodus 22:18; Deuteronomy 98:10; I Samuel 28:7f; II Chronicles 33:6; Isaiah 8:3f.

CHAPTER TWO

CREATION: THE LEGEND OF EVE

If we discard the evolution theory, and accept the Biblical theory of creation, we are still faced with a plethora of interpretations as to how woman began. Contemporary interpretation of the Scriptural references to creation—and especially the creation of woman—is, at best, stagnant and sterile with male domination graphing the degradation of womankind; at worse it is a patent, chauvinistic, overt mis-interpretation perpetuated from time's own beginning.

Much of the contemporary concensus concerning the genesis of womankind is done because of language quali-fiers. The Hebrew language, like most other languages, is distinctly and succinctly male dominated and oriented. This is acutely seen in the *Decalogue*. The Ten Commandments are addressed almost exclusively to the male—especially when seen in the injunction which places woman on the level of any other property: "*do not covet your neighbor's wife, ox, nor ass, manservant, nor maidservant, nor anything that your neighbor possesses.*"[1] The only time a woman is accorded near equality comes with the nearly androgynous Fourth Commandment, which reads: "*Honor your father and your mother that your days may be long upon the land which has been given to you by God.*"[2]

וְנֵם־אָמְנָה אֲחֹתִי בַת־אָבִי הִוא אַךְ לֹא
בַת־אִמֵּי וַתְּהִי־לִי לְאִשָּׁה:

There is truly only one consolation for women in regards to the Ten Commandments. Eventhough theologians and religious commentators have used the commandments and other scriptural passages as "proof" for their claims that women are "naturally" inferior to men, thereby giving the men the "right" to control women in all things by all means: from her style of dressing to possession of her own body. The address of Scripture *is* most definitely directed towards *man*; therefore, in a technically precise reading of the commandments it must be accepted that since they are addressed to *man*, then only *man* can sin—woman, at best, need only honor her father and her mother!

There are problems, however, in approaching the Biblical passages from a literal point of view and interpretation. These problems become especially sharp and critical when approaching the Creation Narrative.

Nowhere in the Creation Narrative is woman subordinate—or endebted—to man. Such a situation can only be *inferred* from the listing of the female after the male; yet, even this is an error, for the key verse (v. 26) uses the word *adham* and it is used generically. *Adham* is both female and male; more precisely *Adham* means "the human race".

This is specified a little further into the telling of the Creation Narrative, for V:3 reads: "*both* male *and* female *God created them.*"

Men and women were created together—not separately and unequally. The commission to have dominion over all things, again, is given jointly: neither male nor female is placed over the other, nor is one subordinate to the other.[3]

In its refined form Judaism implicitly disavows sexism. Yahweh is without sex or sexuality. Yahweh is a god who cannot tolerate a cult of sexuality for Yahweh is one and complete. Yahweh is above sex, sexual distinction, and sexuality in all of its various forms.[4]

The fullness of Yahweh is in being both male and female. Yahweh is androgynous, for Yahweh is the parent who nurtures, admonishes, corrects, punishes, and blesses with equal interest, attention, understanding and compassion for both mortal sexes. It is written: "*I am God [El] and not man [ish], the Holy one in your midst.*"[5]

Yahweh has the attributes of both sexes: both male and female. Yahweh is a dressmaker,[6] a nurse,[7] a supplier of water,[8] a cook and preparer of manna and quail.[9] The god Yahweh even experiences birth pains—and celebrates the joy of giving birth![10] At the same time Yahweh is also a gardener, creator, planeteer, and planter.[11] Yahweh compliments every "male" action with an equal "female" action!

Yahweh does not separate nor differentiate between male and female until Creation Narrative is nearly over: as read in Genesis 2:21-23. Up to that time the two human beings are one: *adham*. Again that particular androgynous word appears and it superbly incorporates the two sexes into one—the way Yahweh viewed them and created them!

Furthermore, the Creation Narrative glorifies woman far more than it praises man! It follows the standard, traditional Yahwist account.

Yahwist literature, like most literatures of the world move towards a climax. Genesis also moves towards a punctuative climax. The story of creation is only a plateau among plateaus—it does not come into its own until woman is created.

When woman is mentioned in the Genesis narrative she is presented last—so that she is first. The Creation Narrative details how the elements are gathered together: it climbs to the separation of the water and the division of the animals. Man is then made. Finally woman is brought into this world which is a park of wonderful wonderment and beauty: the *Gan* or *Eden*: *paradisio*. The story has moved to its climax—not its decline. Woman is the culmination of creation—not the afterthought!

Woman, along with man is the crowning glory of creation—of all civilization. Still we should not read this an *apologia* on the superiority of woman unreachable by man, any more than the past should have translated the Creation Narrative to subordinate woman. The narrative reads: (my translation)

In the beginning God created the heavens and the earth. The earth was without shape and there was nothing on it except for darkness which was upon the waters which were forming. And the mind of God thought of these waters, and said, "Let there be light [and light appeared]. God understood the light and knew it was good and separated time between light and darkness. God called the light "day" and the darkness was called "night"— the light and darkness took place during the first period of creation.

God then said "Let their be a support over the chaos that will separate the waters from a single unit." And God made this vault between the godself and the waters so that the waters would be below the firmament and the godself above the arch. And God called this arch the sky—and this act took the Godhead yet another period of time.

Then God said "Let the waters beneath the sky be gathered together into one place, and let the land which is beneath the waters appear and become dry"—and it occurred:

בְּרֵאשִׁית בָּרָא אֱלֹהִים אֵת הַשָּׁמַיִם וְאֵת הָאָרֶץ: וְהָאָרֶץ הָיְתָה תֹהוּ וָבֹהוּ וְחֹשֶׁךְ עַל־פְּנֵי תְהוֹם וְרוּחַ אֱלֹהִים מְרַחֶפֶת עַל־פְּנֵי הַמָּיִם: וַיֹּאמֶר אֱלֹהִים יְהִי־אוֹר וַיְהִי־אוֹר: וַיַּרְא אֱלֹהִים אֶת־הָאוֹר כִּי־טוֹב וַיַּבְדֵּל אֱלֹהִים בֵּין הָאוֹר וּבֵין הַחֹשֶׁךְ: וַיִּקְרָא אֱלֹהִים לָאוֹר יוֹם וְלַחֹשֶׁךְ קָרָא לָיְלָה וַיְהִי־עֶרֶב וַיְהִי־בֹקֶר יוֹם אֶחָד: פ וַיֹּאמֶר אֱלֹהִים יְהִי רָקִיעַ בְּתוֹךְ הַמָּיִם וִיהִי מַבְדִּיל בֵּין מַיִם לָמָיִם: וַיַּעַשׂ אֱלֹהִים אֶת־הָרָקִיעַ וַיַּבְדֵּל בֵּין הַמַּיִם אֲשֶׁר מִתַּחַת לָרָקִיעַ וּבֵין הַמַּיִם אֲשֶׁר מֵעַל לָרָקִיעַ וַיְהִי־כֵן: וַיִּקְרָא אֱלֹהִים לָרָקִיעַ שָׁמָיִם וַיְהִי־עֶרֶב וַיְהִי־בֹקֶר יוֹם שֵׁנִי: פ וַיֹּאמֶר אֱלֹהִים יִקָּווּ הַמַּיִם מִתַּחַת הַשָּׁמַיִם אֶל־מָקוֹם אֶחָד וְתֵרָאֶה הַיַּבָּשָׁה וַיְהִי־כֵן: וַיִּקְרָא אֱלֹהִים

'Εν ἀρχῇ ἐποίησεν ὁ Θεὸς τὸν οὐρανὸν καὶ τὴν γῆν. Ἡ δὲ γῆ ἦν ἀόρατος, καὶ ἀκατασκεύαστος, καὶ σκότος ἐπάνω τῆς ἀβύσσου· καὶ πνεῦμα Θεοῦ ἐπεφέρετο ἐπάνω τοῦ ὕδατος. Καὶ εἶπεν ὁ Θεός, Γενηθήτω φῶς, καὶ ἐγένετο φῶς. Καὶ εἶδεν ὁ Θεὸς τὸ φῶς, ὅτι καλόν· καὶ διεχώρισεν ὁ Θεὸς ἀνὰ μέσον τοῦ φωτός, καὶ ἀνὰ μέσον τοῦ σκότους. Καὶ ἐκάλεσεν ὁ Θεὸς τὸ φῶς Ἡμέραν, καὶ τὸ σκότος ἐκάλεσε Νύκτα· καὶ ἐγένετο ἑσπέρα, καὶ ἐγένετο πρωί, ἡμέρα μία. Καὶ εἶπεν ὁ Θεός, Γενηθήτω στερέωμα ἐν μέσῳ τοῦ ὕδατος, καὶ ἔστω διαχωρίζον ἀνὰ μέσον ὕδατος καὶ ὕδατος· καὶ ἐγένετο οὕτως. Καὶ ἐποίησεν ὁ Θεὸς τὸ στερέωμα· καὶ διεχώρισεν ὁ Θεὸς ἀνὰ μέσον τοῦ ὕδατος ὃ ἦν ὑποκάτω τοῦ στερεώματος, καὶ ἀνὰ μέσον τοῦ ὕδατος, τοῦ ἐπάνω τοῦ στερεώματος. Καὶ ἐκάλεσεν ὁ Θεὸς τὸ στερέωμα, Οὐρανόν. καὶ εἶδεν ὁ Θεός, ὅτι καλόν· καὶ ἐγένετο ἑσπέρα, καὶ ἐγένετο πρωί, ἡμέρα δευτέρα. Καὶ εἶπεν ὁ Θεός, Συναχθήτω τὸ ὕδωρ τὸ ὑποκάτω τοῦ οὐρανοῦ εἰς συναγωγὴν μίαν, καὶ ὀφθήτω ἡ ξηρά· καὶ ἐγένετο οὕτως· καὶ συνήχθη τὸ ὕδωρ τὸ ὑποκάτω τοῦ οὐρανοῦ εἰς τὰς συναγωγὰς αὐτῶν, καὶ ὤφθη ἡ ξηρά. Καὶ ἐκάλεσεν ὁ Θεὸς τὴν ξηρὰν,

and God called the dry land Earth. The waters which gathered together God called Seas, and God knew it was all good.

God then said, "Let grass appear on the earth, let there appear herbs with seed, and let trees bear fruit individually" for all of these things were already seeds in the earth ready to blossom—and so it occurred. The earth grew grasses and herbs with seeds, and the trees bloomed with fruit (for the fruit seed was in the tree), and various fruits developed; and God understood it was good, and so the third period of time passed.

Then God said, "Let light appear in the dark skies to separate day and night, and let these lights be signs to denote seasons, days, and even years: and let these lights illuminate the earth"—and it occurred with God making two great lights: the largest light to be in the daytime, and the smaller light to shine at night which would be helped with stars God also made.

God put the stars in the heavens so that the earth would have light. They ruled

לַיַּבָּשָׁה אֶרֶץ וּלְמִקְוֵה הַמַּיִם קָרָא יַמִּים וַיַּרְא אֱלֹהִים כִּי־טוֹב : וַיֹּאמֶר אֱלֹהִים תַּדְשֵׁא הָאָרֶץ דֶּשֶׁא עֵשֶׂב מַזְרִיעַ זֶרַע עֵץ פְּרִי עֹשֶׂה פְּרִי לְמִינוֹ אֲשֶׁר זַרְעוֹ־בוֹ עַל־הָאָרֶץ וַיְהִי־כֵן : וַתּוֹצֵא הָאָרֶץ דֶּשֶׁא עֵשֶׂב מַזְרִיעַ זֶרַע לְמִינֵהוּ וְעֵץ עֹשֶׂה־פְּרִי אֲשֶׁר זַרְעוֹ־בוֹ לְמִינֵהוּ וַיַּרְא אֱלֹהִים כִּי־ טוֹב : ' וַיְהִי־עֶרֶב וַיְהִי־בֹקֶר יוֹם שְׁלִישִׁי :
פ וַיֹּאמֶר אֱלֹהִים יְהִי מְאֹרֹת בִּרְקִיעַ הַשָּׁמַיִם לְהַבְדִּיל בֵּין הַיּוֹם וּבֵין הַלָּיְלָה וְהָיוּ לְאֹתֹת וּלְמוֹעֲדִים וּלְיָמִים וְשָׁנִים : וְהָיוּ לִמְאוֹרֹת בִּרְקִיעַ הַשָּׁמַיִם לְהָאִיר עַל־הָאָרֶץ וַיְהִי־כֵן : וַיַּעַשׂ אֱלֹהִים אֶת־שְׁנֵי הַמְּאֹרֹת הַגְּדֹלִים אֶת־ הַמָּאוֹר הַגָּדֹל לְמֶמְשֶׁלֶת הַיּוֹם וְאֶת־הַמָּאוֹר הַקָּטֹן לְמֶמְשֶׁלֶת הַלַּיְלָה וְאֵת הַכּוֹכָבִים :

Γῆν, καὶ τὰ συστήματα τῶν ὑδάτων ἐκάλεσε Θαλάσσας· καὶ εἶδεν ὁ Θεὸς, ὅτι καλόν. Καὶ εἶπεν ὁ Θεὸς, Βλαστησάτω ἡ γῆ βοτάνην χόρτου σπεῖρον σπέρμα κατὰ γένος καὶ καθ' ὁμοιότητα, καὶ ξύλον κάρπιμον ποιοῦν καρπόν, οὗ τὸ σπέρμα αὐτοῦ ἐν αὐτῷ κατὰ γένος ἐπὶ τῆς γῆς· καὶ ἐγένετο οὕτως. Καὶ ἐξήνεγκεν ἡ γῆ βοτάνην χόρτου σπεῖρον σπέρμα κατὰ γένος καὶ καθ' ὁμοιότητα, καὶ ξύλον κάρπιμον ποιοῦν καρπὸν, οὗ τὸ σπέρμα αὐτοῦ ἐν αὐτῷ κατὰ γένος ἐπὶ τῆς γῆς· καὶ εἶδεν ὁ·Θεὸς, ὅτι καλόν. Καὶ ἐγένετο ἑσπέρα, καὶ ἐγένετο πρωί, ἡμέρα τρίτη. Καὶ εἶπεν ὁ Θεὸς, Γενηθήτωσαν φωστῆρες ἐν τῷ στερεώματι τοῦ οὐρανοῦ εἰς φαῦσιν ἐπὶ τῆς γῆς, τοῦ διαχωρίζειν ἀνὰ μέσον τῆς ἡμέρας καὶ ἀνὰ μέσον τῆς νυκτός· καὶ ἔστωσαν εἰς σημεῖα, καὶ εἰς καιρούς, καὶ εἰς ἡμέρας, καὶ εἰς ἐνιαυτούς. Καὶ ἔστωσαν εἰς φαῦσιν ἐν τῷ στερεώματι τοῦ οὐρανοῦ, ὥστε φαίνειν ἐπὶ τῆς γῆς· καὶ ἐγένετο οὕτως. Καὶ ἐποίησεν ὁ Θεὸς τοὺς δύο φωστῆρας τοὺς μεγάλους, τὸν φωστῆρα τὸν μέγαν εἰς ἀρχὰς τῆς ἡμέρας, καὶ τὸν φωστῆρα τὸν ἐλάσσω εἰς ἀρχὰς τῆς νυκτός, καὶ τοὺς ἀστέρας.

12

over the day and the night and divided the light from the darkness. God knew that it was good. All of this took a fourth period of time.

God then said, "Let the waters be filled with every living creature, and let birds fly in the sky overhead." God then created great sea-animals as well as a multitude of other sea creatures and they reproduced their species; and God did the same with every fowl that flies and they reproduced. And God was pleased.

God then commanded the waters to be filled with living creatures of every kind, and also caused birds to fly in the sky above the earth. And this took place during the fifth time period.

God then required the earth to yeild all forms of life from cattle, to creeping things, and even beasts. Each of the creatures were unique and separate as were all the creeping things—and God was pleased.

Then God said, let us create beings fashioned after our image—after the divine likeness and let *them* have dominion over the fish of the sea, and over the birds of the air and over the cattle, and over all of the earth, and over

וַיִּתֵּן אֹתָם אֱלֹהִים בִּרְקִיעַ הַשָּׁמָיִם לְהָאִיר עַל־הָאָרֶץ : וְלִמְשֹׁל בַּיּוֹם וּבַלַּיְלָה וּלֲהַבְדִּיל בֵּין הָאוֹר וּבֵין הַחֹשֶׁךְ וַיַּרְא אֱלֹהִים כִּי־טוֹב : וַיְהִי־עֶרֶב וַיְהִי־בֹקֶר יוֹם רְבִיעִי : פ וַיֹּאמֶר אֱלֹהִים יִשְׁרְצוּ הַמַּיִם שֶׁרֶץ נֶפֶשׁ חַיָּה וְעוֹף יְעוֹפֵף עַל־הָאָרֶץ עַל־פְּנֵי רְקִיעַ הַשָּׁמָיִם : וַיִּבְרָא אֱלֹהִים אֶת־הַתַּנִּינִם הַגְּדֹלִים . וְאֵת כָּל־נֶפֶשׁ הַחַיָּה הָרֹמֶשֶׂת אֲשֶׁר שָׁרְצוּ הַמַּיִם לְמִינֵהֶם וְאֵת כָּל־עוֹף כָּנָף לְמִינֵהוּ וַיַּרְא אֱלֹהִים כִּי־טוֹב : וַיְבָרֶךְ אֹתָם אֱלֹהִים לֵאמֹר פְּרוּ וּרְבוּ וּמִלְאוּ אֶת־הַמַּיִם בַּיַּמִּים וְהָעוֹף יִרֶב בָּאָרֶץ : וַיְהִי־עֶרֶב וַיְהִי־בֹקֶר יוֹם חֲמִישִׁי : פ · וַיֹּאמֶר אֱלֹהִים תּוֹצֵא הָאָרֶץ נֶפֶשׁ חַיָּה לְמִינָהּ בְּהֵמָה וָרֶמֶשׂ וְחַיְתוֹ־אֶרֶץ לְמִינָהּ וַיְהִי־כֵן : וַיַּעַשׂ אֱלֹהִים אֶת־חַיַּת הָאָרֶץ לְמִינָהּ וְאֶת־הַבְּהֵמָה לְמִינָהּ וְאֵת כָּל־רֶמֶשׂ הָאֲדָמָה לְמִינֵהוּ וַיַּרְא אֱלֹהִים כִּי־טוֹב : וַיֹּאמֶר אֱלֹהִים נַעֲשֶׂה אָדָם בְּצַלְמֵנוּ כִּדְמוּתֵנוּ וְיִרְדּוּ בִדְגַת הַיָּם וּבְעוֹף הַשָּׁמַיִם וּבַבְּהֵמָה וּבְכָל־הָאָרֶץ וּבְכָל־הָרֶמֶשׂ הָרֹמֵשׂ

Καὶ ἔθετο αὐτοὺς ὁ Θεὸς ἐν τῷ στερεώματι τοῦ οὐρανοῦ, ὥστε φαίνειν ἐπὶ τῆς γῆς, Καὶ ἄρχειν τῆς ἡμέρας καὶ τῆς νυκτός, καὶ διαχωρίζειν ἀνὰ μέσον τοῦ φωτὸς καὶ ἀνὰ μέσον τοῦ σκότους· καὶ εἶδεν ὁ Θεὸς, ὅτι καλόν. Καὶ ἐγένετο ἑσπέρα, καὶ ἐγένετο πρωΐ, ἡμέρα τετάρτη. Καὶ εἶπεν ὁ Θεὸς, Ἐξαγαγέτω τὰ ὕδατα ἑρπετὰ ψυχῶν ζωσῶν, καὶ πετεινὰ πετόμενα ἐπὶ τῆς γῆς κατὰ τὸ στερέωμα τοῦ οὐρανοῦ· καὶ ἐγένετο οὕτως. Καὶ ἐποίησεν ὁ Θεὸς τὰ κήτη τὰ μεγάλα, καὶ πᾶσαν ψυχὴν ζώων ἑρπετῶν, ἃ ἐξήγαγε τὰ ὕδατα κατὰ γένη αὐτῶν, καὶ πᾶν πετεινὸν πτερωτὸν κατὰ γένος· καὶ εἶδεν ὁ Θεὸς, ὅτι καλά. Καὶ εὐλόγησεν αὐτὰ ὁ Θεὸς, λέγων, Αὐξάνεσθε καὶ πληθύνεσθε, καὶ πληρώσατε τὰ ὕδατα ἐν ταῖς θαλάσσαις, καὶ τὰ πετεινὰ πληθυνέσθωσαν ἐπὶ τῆς γῆς, Καὶ ἐγένετο ἑσπέρα, καὶ ἐγένετο πρωΐ, ἡμέρα πέμπτη. Καὶ εἶπεν ὁ Θεὸς, Ἐξα- γαγέτω ἡ γῆ ψυχὴν ζῶσαν κατὰ γένος, τετράποδα, καὶ ἑρπετὰ, καὶ θηρία τῆς γῆς κατὰ γένος· καὶ ἐγένετο οὕτως. Καὶ ἐποίησεν ὁ Θεὸς τὰ θηρία τῆς γῆς κατὰ γένος, καὶ τὰ κτήνη κατὰ γένος αὐτῶν, καὶ πάντα τὰ ἑρπετὰ τῆς γῆς κατὰ γένος· καὶ εἶδεν ὁ Θεὸς, ὅτι καλά. Καὶ εἶπεν ὁ Θεὸς, Ποιήσωμεν ἄνθρωπον κατ᾽ εἰκόνα ἡμετέραν καὶ καθ᾽ ὁμοίωσιν· καὶ ἀρχέτωσαν τῶν ἰχθύων τῆς θαλάσσης, καὶ τῶν πετεινῶν τοῦ οὐρανοῦ, καὶ τῶν κτηνῶν, καὶ πάσης τῆς γῆς, καὶ πάντων τῶν ἑρπετῶν τῶν ἑρπόντων ἐπὶ τῆς γῆς. Καὶ ἐποίησεν ὁ Θεὸς

every creeping thing that does creep upon the earth. So God created humankind in the divine image: and they were created *male and female*. God blessed them and told them "Reproduce your own kind and fill the earth so that you may make it subject to your needs, for you are to have control over the fish of the sea, the birds of the air, and over all other living things, which live on and over the earth."

God also said, "See! I have given you herbs of every kind and they all have seeds which will reproduce. Also there are trees which will produce various fruits. You are to eat of these gifts."

God was pleased. It was the sixth day.

עַל־הָאָרֶץ : וַיִּבְרָא אֱלֹהִים ׀ אֶת־הָאָדָם בְּצַלְמוֹ בְּצֶלֶם אֱלֹהִים בָּרָא אֹתוֹ זָכָר וּנְקֵבָה בָּרָא אֹתָם : וַיְבָרֶךְ אֹתָם אֱלֹהִים וַיֹּאמֶר לָהֶם אֱלֹהִים פְּרוּ וּרְבוּ וּמִלְאוּ אֶת־הָאָרֶץ וְכִבְשֻׁהָ וּרְדוּ בִּדְגַת הַיָּם וּבְעוֹף הַשָּׁמַיִם וּבְכָל־חַיָּה הָרֹמֶשֶׂת עַל־ הָאָרֶץ : וַיֹּאמֶר אֱלֹהִים הִנֵּה נָתַתִּי לָכֶם אֶת־כָּל־עֵשֶׂב ׀ זֹרֵעַ זֶרַע אֲשֶׁר עַל־פְּנֵי כָל־הָאָרֶץ וְאֶת־כָּל־הָעֵץ אֲשֶׁר־בּוֹ פְרִי־עֵץ זֹרֵעַ זָרַע לָכֶם יִהְיֶה לְאָכְלָה : וּלְכָל־ חַיַּת הָאָרֶץ וּלְכָל־עוֹף הַשָּׁמַיִם וּלְכֹל ׀ רוֹמֵשׂ עַל־הָאָרֶץ אֲשֶׁר־בּוֹ נֶפֶשׁ חַיָּה אֶת־כָּל־יֶרֶק עֵשֶׂב לְאָכְלָה וַיְהִי־כֵן : וַיַּרְא אֱלֹהִים אֶת־כָּל־אֲשֶׁר עָשָׂה וְהִנֵּה־טוֹב מְאֹד וַיְהִי־עֶרֶב וַיְהִי־בֹקֶר יוֹם הַשִּׁשִּׁי : פ

τὸν ἄνθρωπον, κατ' εἰκόνα Θεοῦ ἐποίησεν αὐτόν· ἄρσεν καὶ θῆλυ ἐποίησεν αὐτούς. Καὶ εὐλό- γησεν αὐτοὺς ὁ Θεός, λέγων, Αὐξάνεσθε καὶ πλη- θύνεσθε, καὶ πληρώσατε τὴν γῆν, καὶ κατακυριεύσατε αὐτῆς, καὶ ἄρχετε τῶν ἰχθύων τῆς θαλάσσης, καὶ τῶν πετεινῶν τοῦ οὐρανοῦ, καὶ πάντων τῶν κτηνῶν, καὶ πάσης τῆς γῆς, καὶ πάντων τῶν ἑρπετῶν τῶν ἑρπόντων ἐπὶ τῆς γῆς. Καὶ εἶπεν ὁ Θεός, Ἰδοὺ δέδωκα ὑμῖν πάντα χόρτον σπόριμον σπεῖ- ρον σπέρμα, ὅ ἐστιν ἐπάνω πάσης τῆς γῆς· καὶ πᾶν ξύλον, ὃ ἔχει ἐν ἑαυτῷ καρπὸν σπέρματος σπορίμου, ὑμῖν ἔσται εἰς βρῶσιν· Καὶ πᾶσι τοῖς θηρίοις τῆς γῆς, καὶ πᾶσι τοῖς πετεινοῖς τοῦ οὐρανοῦ, καὶ παντὶ ἑρπετῷ ἕρποντι ἐπὶ τῆς γῆς, ὃ ἔχει ἐν ἑαυτῷ ψυχὴν ζωῆς, καὶ πάντα χόρτον χλωρὸν εἰς βρῶσιν· καὶ ἐγένετο οὕτως. ... Καὶ εἶδεν ὁ Θεὸς τὰ πάντα, ὅσα ἐποίησε· καὶ ἰδοὺ καλὰ λίαν. Καὶ ἐγένετο ἑσπέρα, καὶ ἐγένετο πρωὶ, ἡμέρα ἕκτη.

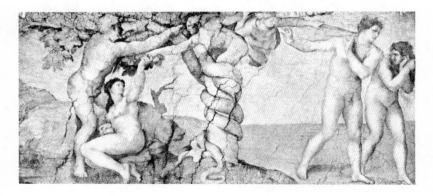

14

Man and woman are equals throughout the first account of creation (Genesis 1).

The only time man appears prior to woman is in Genesis 2—an account, by all indications, written much later than the first record. It translates as:

The heavens and the earth were finished. So too were all the other spheres.

On the seventh day [or period of time] God stopped working and rested—viewing all the things that were made.

God blessed that special day: the seventh, and God decided that it would always be special since it marked the end of the work of creation: which included the creation of the sky and the earth, of every plant in the fields on the earth and also of every herb which grew from seeds—but none

וַיְכֻלּ֣וּ הַשָּׁמַ֥יִם וְהָאָ֖רֶץ וְכָל־צְבָאָֽם׃
וַיְכַ֤ל אֱלֹהִים֙ בַּיֹּ֣ום הַשְּׁבִיעִ֔י מְלַאכְתֹּ֖ו
אֲשֶׁ֣ר עָשָׂ֑ה וַיִּשְׁבֹּת֙ בַּיֹּ֣ום הַשְּׁבִיעִ֔י מִכָּל־
מְלַאכְתֹּ֖ו אֲשֶׁ֥ר עָשָֽׂה׃ וַיְבָ֤רֶךְ אֱלֹהִים֙
אֶת־יֹ֣ום הַשְּׁבִיעִ֔י וַיְקַדֵּ֖שׁ אֹתֹ֑ו כִּ֣י בֹ֤ו שָׁבַת֙
מִכָּל־מְלַאכְתֹּ֔ו אֲשֶׁר־בָּרָ֥א אֱלֹהִ֖ים לַעֲשֹֽׂות׃ פ
אֵ֣לֶּה תֹולְדֹ֤ות הַשָּׁמַ֙יִם֙ וְהָאָ֔רֶץ
בְּהִבָּֽרְאָ֑ם בְּיֹ֗ום עֲשֹׂ֛ות יְהוָ֥ה אֱלֹהִ֖ים אֶ֥רֶץ
וְשָׁמָֽיִם׃ וְכֹ֣ל ׀ שִׂ֣יחַ הַשָּׂדֶ֗ה טֶ֚רֶם יִֽהְיֶ֣ה
בָאָ֔רֶץ וְכָל־עֵ֥שֶׂב הַשָּׂדֶ֖ה טֶ֣רֶם יִצְמָ֑ח
כִּי֩ לֹ֨א הִמְטִ֜יר יְהוָ֤ה אֱלֹהִים֙ עַל־הָאָ֔רֶץ
וְאָדָ֣ם אַ֔יִן לַֽעֲבֹ֖ד אֶת־הָֽאֲדָמָֽה׃ וְאֵ֖ד

Θεὸς ἐν τῇ ἡμέρᾳ τῇ ἕκτῃ τὰ ἔργα αὐτοῦ ἃ
ἐποίησε· καὶ κατέπαυσε τῇ ἡμέρᾳ τῇ ἑβδόμῃ ἀπὸ
πάντων τῶν ἔργων αὐτοῦ, ὧν ἐποίησε. Καὶ
εὐλόγησεν ὁ Θεὸς τὴν ἡμέραν τὴν ἑβδόμην,
καὶ ἡγίασεν αὐτήν, ὅτι ἐν αὐτῇ κατέπαυσεν

ἀπὸ πάντων τῶν ἔργων αὐτοῦ, ὧν ἤρξατο ὁ Θεὸς
ποιῆσαι. Αὕτη ἡ βίβλος γενέσεως οὐρανοῦ καὶ

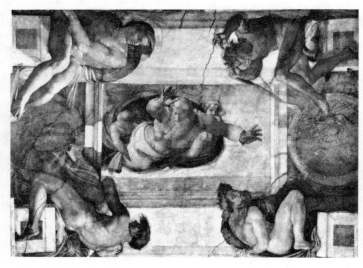

which developed before the rains came for God had not yet caused it to rain upon the earth and there were no people to till the ground so that the seeds could grow. So God created man which was made out of the dust of the earth; God then breathed into man's nostrils the breath of life, and man lived.

God then created a garden eastward of Eden where he put the man he had formed. To make it a garden God made trees grow of every kind. They were not only beautiful to see but were filled with good food. In the center of the park was a tree of life which held all knowledge of both good and evil. A river flowed out of Eden to water this garden—and afterwards it separated into four directions: the first named Pison which flows throughout Havilah where there is gold (and that gold is good and there is also bedellium and onyx). The name of the second river is Gihon, and it flows throughout the entire land of Ethiopia south. And the name of the third river is Hiddekel which goes eastward towards Assyria, The fourth river is the Euphrates.

נַעֲלֶה מִן־הָאָרֶץ וְהִשְׁקָה אֶת־כָּל־פְּנֵי הָאֲדָמָה : ⁷ וַיִּיצֶר יְהוָֹה אֱלֹהִים אֶת־הָאָדָם עָפָר מִן־הָאֲדָמָה וַיִּפַּח בְּאַפָּיו נִשְׁמַת חַיִּים נַיְהִי הָאָדָם לְנֶפֶשׁ חַיָּה : וַיִּטַּע יְהוָֹה אֱלֹהִים גַּן־בְּעֵדֶן מִקֶּדֶם וַיָּשֶׂם שָׁם אֶת־הָאָדָם אֲשֶׁר יָצָר : וַיַּצְמַח יְהוָֹה אֱלֹהִים מִן־הָאֲדָמָה כָּל־עֵץ נֶחְמָד לְמַרְאֶה וְטוֹב לְמַאֲכָל וְעֵץ הַחַיִּים בְּתוֹךְ הַגָּן וְעֵץ הַדַּעַת טוֹב וָרָע : וְנָהָר יֹצֵא מֵעֵדֶן לְהַשְׁקוֹת אֶת־הַגָּן וּמִשָּׁם יִפָּרֵד וְהָיָה לְאַרְבָּעָה רָאשִׁים : שֵׁם הָאֶחָד פִּישׁוֹן הוּא הַסֹּבֵב אֵת כָּל־אֶרֶץ הַחֲוִילָה אֲשֶׁר שָׁם הַזָּהָב : וּזְהַב הָאָרֶץ הַהִוא טוֹב שָׁם הַבְּדֹלַח וְאֶבֶן הַשֹּׁהַם : וְשֵׁם־הַנָּהָר הַשֵּׁנִי גִּיחוֹן הוּא הַסּוֹבֵב אֵת כָּל־אֶרֶץ כּוּשׁ : וְשֵׁם־הַנָּהָר הַשְּׁלִישִׁי חִדֶּקֶל הוּא הַהֹלֵךְ קִדְמַת אַשּׁוּר וְהַנָּהָר הָרְבִיעִי הוּא פְרָת : וַיִּקַּח יְהוָֹה אֱלֹהִים אֶת־הָאָדָם

γῆς, ὅτε ἐγένετο· ᾖ ἡμέρᾳ ἐποίησε Κύριος ὁ Θεὸς τὸν οὐρανὸν καὶ τὴν γῆν, Καὶ πᾶν χλωρὸν ἀγροῦ πρὸ τοῦ γενέσθαι ἐπὶ τῆς γῆς, καὶ πάντα χόρτον ἀγροῦ πρὸ τοῦ ἀνατεῖλαι· οὐ γὰρ ἔβρεξεν ὁ Θεὸς ἐπὶ τὴν γῆν, καὶ ἄνθρωπος οὐκ ἦν ἐργάζεσθαι αὐτήν. Πηγὴ δὲ ἀνέβαινεν ἐκ τῆς γῆς, καὶ ἐπότιζε πᾶν τὸ πρόσωπον τῆς γῆς. Καὶ ἔπλασεν ὁ Θεὸς τὸν ἄνθρωπον, χοῦν ἀπὸ τῆς γῆς, καὶ ἐνεφύσησεν εἰς τὸ πρόσωπον αὐτοῦ πνοὴν ζωῆς, καὶ ἐγένετο ὁ ἄνθρωπος εἰς ψυχὴν ζῶσαν. Καὶ ἐφύτευσεν ὁ Θεὸς παράδεισον ἐν Ἐδὲμ κατὰ ἀνατολάς, καὶ ἔθετο ἐκεῖ τὸν ἄνθρωπον, ὃν ἔπλασε.

Καὶ ἐξανέτειλεν ὁ Θεὸς ἔτι ἐκ τῆς γῆς πᾶν ξύλον ὡραῖον εἰς ὅρασιν καὶ καλὸν εἰς βρῶσιν· καὶ τὸ ξύλον τῆς ζωῆς ἐν μέσῳ τοῦ παραδείσου, καὶ τὸ ξύλον τοῦ εἰδέναι γνωστὸν καλοῦ καὶ πονηροῦ. Ποταμὸς δὲ ἐκπορεύεται ἐξ Ἐδὲμ ποτίζειν τὸν παράδεισον· ἐκεῖθεν ἀφορίζεται εἰς τέσσαρας ἀρχάς. Ὄνομα τῷ ἑνὶ, Φισών· οὗτος ὁ κυκλῶν πᾶσαν τὴν γῆν Εὐιλὰτ, ἐκεῖ οὗ ἐστι τὸ χρυσίον. Τὸ δὲ χρυσίον τῆς γῆς ἐκείνης καλόν· καὶ ἐκεῖ ἐστιν ὁ ἄνθραξ καὶ ὁ λίθος ὁ πράσινος. Καὶ ὄνομα τῷ ποταμῷ τῷ δευτέρῳ, Γεών· οὗτος ὁ κυκλῶν πᾶσαν τὴν γῆν Αἰθιοπίας. Καὶ ὁ ποταμὸς ὁ τρίτος Τίγρις, οὗτος ὁ προπορευόμενος κατέναντι Ἀσσυρίων. Ὁ δὲ ποταμὸς ὁ τέταρτος, Εὐφράτης. Καὶ

16

God took man to this garden to take care of it. God had one paramount instruction: "You may eat of every fruit of every tree as much as you wish—but do not eat of the tree of knowledge which would let you know the difference between good and evil—for if you do, on that day, you will lose my favor."

God worried about man living alone, and said, "It isn't good that man is alone. I will make him a helper."

God formed out of the ground every beast of the field, and every bird of the air, and brought them to the man to see what he would call them. Whatever the man called them that was the creature's name from that time forward.

The man gave names to all the cattle, and to every bird of the air, and to every beast of the field—but still the man did not have a helper.

[Seeing this] God caused man to fall into a deep sleep, during which time God took one of man's ribs, and then closed up the flesh from which the rib was taken.

From the man's rib

וַיַּנִּחֵהוּ בְגַן־עֵדֶן לְעָבְדָהּ וּלְשָׁמְרָהּ : וַיְצַו
יְהֹוָה אֱלֹהִים עַל־הָאָדָם לֵאמֹר מִכֹּל
עֵץ־הַגָּן אָכֹל תֹּאכֵל : וּמֵעֵץ הַדַּעַת
טוֹב וָרָע לֹא תֹאכַל מִמֶּנּוּ כִּי בְּיוֹם אֲכָלְךָ
מִמֶּנּוּ מוֹת תָּמוּת : וַיֹּאמֶר יְהֹוָה אֱלֹהִים
לֹא־טוֹב הֱיוֹת הָאָדָם לְבַדּוֹ אֶעֱשֶׂה־לּוֹ
עֵזֶר כְּנֶגְדּוֹ : וַיִּצֶר יְהֹוָה אֱלֹהִים מִן
הָאֲדָמָה כָּל־חַיַּת הַשָּׂדֶה וְאֵת כָּל־עוֹף
הַשָּׁמַיִם וַיָּבֵא אֶל־הָאָדָם לִרְאוֹת מַה־
יִּקְרָא־לוֹ וְכֹל אֲשֶׁר יִקְרָא־לוֹ הָאָדָם נֶפֶשׁ
חַיָּה הוּא שְׁמוֹ : וַיִּקְרָא הָאָדָם שֵׁמוֹת
לְכָל־הַבְּהֵמָה וּלְעוֹף הַשָּׁמַיִם וּלְכֹל חַיַּת
הַשָּׂדֶה וּלְאָדָם לֹא־מָצָא עֵזֶר כְּנֶגְדּוֹ :
וַיַּפֵּל יְהֹוָה אֱלֹהִים תַּרְדֵּמָה עַל־הָאָדָם
וַיִּישָׁן וַיִּקַּח אַחַת מִצַּלְעֹתָיו וַיִּסְגֹּר בָּשָׂר
תַּחְתֶּנָּה : וַיִּבֶן יְהֹוָה אֱלֹהִים אֶת־הַצֵּלָע
אֲשֶׁר־לָקַח מִן־הָאָדָם לְאִשָּׁה וַיְבִאֶהָ אֶל־

Ἔλαβε Κύριος ὁ Θεὸς τὸν ἄνθρωπον ὃν ἔπλασε, καὶ ἔθετο αὐτὸν ἐν τῷ παραδείσῳ τῆς τρυφῆς, ἐργάζεσθαι αὐτὸν καὶ φυλάσσειν. Καὶ ἐνετείλατο Κύριος ὁ Θεὸς τῷ Ἀδάμ, λέγων, Ἀπὸ παντὸς ξύλου τοῦ ἐν τῷ παραδείσῳ βρώσει φαγῇ· Ἀπὸ δὲ τοῦ ξύλου τοῦ γινώσκειν καλὸν καὶ πονηρόν, οὐ φάγεσθε ἀπ' αὐτοῦ· ᾗ δ' ἂν ἡμέρᾳ φάγητε ἀπ' αὐτοῦ, θανάτῳ ἀποθανεῖσθε. Καὶ εἶπε Κύριος ὁ Θεός, Οὐ καλὸν εἶναι τὸν ἄνθρωπον μόνον· ποιήσωμεν αὐτῷ βοηθὸν κατ' αὐτόν. Καὶ ἔπλασεν ὁ Θεὸς ἔτι ἐκ τῆς γῆς πάντα τὰ θηρία τοῦ ἀγροῦ, καὶ πάντα τὰ πετεινὰ τοῦ οὐρανοῦ, κα' ἤγαγεν αὐτὰ πρὸς τὸν Ἀδάμ, ἰδεῖν τί καλέσει αὐτά· καὶ πᾶν ὃ ἐὰν ἐκάλεσεν αὐτὸ Ἀδὰμ ψυχὴν ζῶσαν, τοῦτο ὄνομα αὐτῷ. Καὶ ἐκάλεσεν Ἀδὰμ ὀνόματα πᾶσι τοῖς κτήνεσι καὶ πᾶσι τοῖς πετεινοῖς τοῦ οὐρανοῦ, καὶ πᾶσι τοῖς θηρίοις τοῦ ἀγροῦ· τῷ δὲ Ἀδὰμ οὐχ εὑρέθη βοηθὸς ὅμοιος αὐτῷ. Καὶ ἐπέβαλεν ὁ Θεὸς ἔκστασιν ἐπὶ τὸν Ἀδάμ, καὶ ὕπνωσε· καὶ ἔλαβε μίαν τῶν πλευρῶν αὐτοῦ, καὶ ἀνεπλήρωσε σάρκα ἀντ' αὐτῆς. Καὶ ᾠκοδόμησεν ὁ Θεὸς τὴν πλευράν, ἣν ἔλαβεν ἀπὸ τοῦ Ἀδάμ, εἰς γυναῖκα, καὶ ἤγαγεν αὐτὴν πρὸς τὸν Ἀδάμ. Καὶ εἶπεν Ἀδάμ, Τοῦτο νῦν

God fashioned a woman—and then brought her to the man.

The man said, "This is me: bone of my bone, flesh of my flesh. She shall be called *woman* since she was taken out of *man*."

[Therefore a man shall leave his father and mother, and shall take a wife, and become as one person]

They were both naked both the man and the woman. They were not ashamed.

הָאָדָם : וַיֹּאמֶר הָאָדָם זֹאת הַפַּעַם עֶצֶם
מֵעֲצָמַי וּבָשָׂר מִבְּשָׂרִי לְזֹאת יִקָּרֵא אִשָּׁה
כִּי מֵאִישׁ לֻקֳחָה־זֹּאת : עַל־כֵּן יַעֲזָב־אִישׁ
אֶת־אָבִיו וְאֶת־אִמּוֹ וְדָבַק בְּאִשְׁתּוֹ וְהָיוּ
לְבָשָׂר אֶחָד : וַיִּהְיוּ שְׁנֵיהֶם עֲרוּמִּים
הָאָדָם וְאִשְׁתּוֹ וְלֹא יִתְבֹּשָׁשׁוּ :

ὀστοῦν ἐκ τῶν ὀστέων μου, καὶ σάρξ ἐκ τῆς σαρκὸς
μου· αὕτη κληθήσεται Γυνή, ὅτι ἐκ τοῦ ἀνδρὸς αὐτῆς
ἐλήφθη. Ἕνεκεν τούτου καταλείψει ἄνθρωπος
τὸν πατέρα αὐτοῦ καὶ τὴν μητέρα, καὶ προσκολλη-
θήσεται πρὸς τὴν γυναῖκα αὐτοῦ· καὶ ἔσονται οἱ
δύο εἰς σάρκα μίαν. Καὶ ἦσαν οἱ δύο γυμνοί,
ὅ τε Ἀδὰμ καὶ ἡ γυνὴ αὐτοῦ, καὶ οὐκ ᾐσχύνοντο.

What is noteworthy is the uniquess of each account. Genesis 1 details the actual creation. Genesis 1 has man and woman created at the same time. Both are equals.

Genesis 2 begins with creation nearly completed—all that is lacking is humankind: man and woman. God, in Genesis 2, is not the kind, loving, compassionate God in Genesis 1; instead the God of Genesis 2 is a selfish God that creates *man* to take care of his park. Only after *man is created to take care of the park, does God worry that man might become lonely—possibly bitter* (but to what end—certainly man could not quit, leave the garden, and seek new employment!) To stop any problem before it begins God decides to make a *helper* for man—this helper need not have been a woman— the text merely states "helper" (or "help-mate") without a sexual qualifier. That it proves to be a woman is incidental. The creation of woman is far more significant, for she is created to work with the man at keeping the garden in the manner desired by God.

God also is anything but truly "godly" in the sense of omnipotence—he doesn't spontaneously fashion man or woman, but forms man out of the ground—and fashions woman out of the rib of man—which he has to take almost surgically: God has to close up the flesh from where the rib was removed. Obviously this is a later record when incisions are known. A further testimony that this chapter or version of the Creation Narrative came at a far later date is verse 24: "Therefore shall a man leave his father and mother...." This is preaching—or commentary—quite outside of the basic development of the story.

The one thing which cannot be gainsaid, however, is even in Genesis 2 man and woman are equals and the very zenith of creation. Genesis 2:18 and 20 uses the two words which are dependent upon one another: *neged* and *ezer*, which together—as they must be—connote equality.

If man was truly superior to woman, then he would have to have had an active—and intimate—role in the creation of woman. This is not the case—according to either Creation Narrative. In Genesis 2 man is made to fall into a deep sleep. When he is asleep—and only when he is asleep—does God—with absolutely no assistance from man—create woman. Man, therefore, has no control over creation and the existence of woman. The intent is obvious—God intended man and woman to be equal.

To argue that man is superior inasmuch as he was created first can also be readily discarded. All that is essential is to look at the elements used by God in the act of creation.

Man was created from the most fragile of all material: dust. Woman was created from the uniquely strong and sturdy substance: a rib—which required *divine* and not mortal labor to fashion.

Another key factor is that no where in Genesis 2 is man made or acknowledged to be superior to the woman. She is to be his helper—but a help*mate*, which means equal.

Furthermore, no where does man demonstrate any great strength or resolve. Independence is totally lacking. He is neither aggressive, nor is he dominate. Rather man remains silent and passive while God plans and interprets his existence and future. Even in the naming of the animals—that is done only on the sufferance of God. God determined man would name the creatures of the earth and instructed man in his duty—man did not tell God the creatures name first.

On the other hand, woman is far different than man. She is *rib* which means solidarity and equality:[12]

וַיֹּאמֶר הָאָדָם זֹאת הַפַּעַם עֶצֶם מֵעֲצָמַי וּבָשָׂר מִבְּשָׂרִי לְזֹאת יִקָּרֵא אִשָּׁה כִּי מֵאִישׁ לֻקֳחָה־זֹּאת:

She is *ishshah* (woman) and the man is *ish*: gaining in strength and importance only when the two are interrelated and interdependent as one. Furthermore, in this key passage she is called *ishshah* by God—not by man. No where is she addressed as *ishshah* by man. Neither the noun nor the verb *name* is in the creation poem. Instead this passage reads: "*she shall be called* (kara)". Kara is a verb which does not function as a synonym for "name" It is idential in meaning and in usage to that passage in Genesis 2:19-20. [13]

Another critical point is the word "*woman*". "*Woman*" is not a name. It is a common noun—not a proper noun. It designates gender only.

Woman might be seen as superior to man in the story of the Temptation. Only she is confronted by the serpent. The serpent speaks only to her. The serpent at no place, nor at any time addresses the man or converses with the man.

Throughout the account of the Temptation Narrative, woman is pictured as more ambitious—and more inquisitive than man. It is the woman—not the man—who is intelligent and aggressive. The man is silent and passive.[14]

The Temptation Narrative presents yet another side to the complex picture of woman. She is a wise person—truly a *homo sapien*—and her wisdom is uncanny and it is unheralded.

Woman appears to be the theologian. She knows and is able to quote scripture—and she is able to respond intelligently to quotations thrown back to her by the serpent who is equally familiar and comfortable with scripture. Furthermore, woman is able to interpret scripture. She demonstrates a powerful and masterful understanding of fine hermeneutic points of scripture and its subsequent debates.

Woman is also ambitious. She covets the tree which is the source of all knowledge and wisdom (*haskil*).

Woman is fully aware of her act—while man still huddles in awe and a state of semiconsciousness and quasiawareness. Seeking to learn even more, it is again woman that is quick to take "the forbidden fruit". And she eats it without regret.

It is woman alone that takes this initiative. She does not seek out the advise nor the consent of the man. She is independent and she wants to grow mentally into a more full awareness of the beauties of reality. She is not afraid.

Woman is independent. Man is silent, bland, passive, dependent, and the recipient. He followers her instruction and her initiative: she is in control in a near matriarchal sense (as was the case in so many early societies—especially those in fertile areas of the ancient Near East as was the situation in early Egypt!). All of this is codified and canonized in the brilliant yet simple statement: *"she also gave some to her husband—and he did eat of it."* The text is clear:

It was that the serpent was more subtle than any beast of the field which the Godhead had made, and the serpent said to the woman, "Hasn't God said that you shall eat of every tree of the garden?"

The woman responded, saying to the serpent, "We may eat of the fruit of the trees of the garden except for the fruit of the tree which is in the middle of the garden, for God warned us, saying, 'You shall not eat of it, nor shall you touch it. Otherwise you will die."

The serpent replied to the woman [only], "You most assuredly will not die, [for it is a ruse] for God knows that the day you eat of that special fruit you will acquire all knowledge and be like the very gods: knowing good and evil."

And then the woman saw that the tree was filled with good fruit—fruit that was most pleasant to the eye—and know-

וְהַנָּחָשׁ הָיָה עָרוּם מִכֹּל חַיַּת הַשָּׂדֶה אֲשֶׁר עָשָׂה יְהוָה אֱלֹהִים וַיֹּאמֶר אֶל־הָאִשָּׁה אַף כִּי־אָמַר אֱלֹהִים לֹא תֹאכְלוּ מִכֹּל עֵץ הַגָּן: ² וַתֹּאמֶר הָאִשָּׁה אֶל־הַנָּחָשׁ מִפְּרִי עֵץ־הַגָּן נֹאכֵל: ³ וּמִפְּרִי הָעֵץ אֲשֶׁר בְּתוֹךְ־הַגָּן אָמַר אֱלֹהִים לֹא תֹאכְלוּ מִמֶּנּוּ וְלֹא תִגְּעוּ בּוֹ פֶּן־תְּמֻתוּן: ⁴ וַיֹּאמֶר הַנָּחָשׁ אֶל־הָאִשָּׁה לֹא־מוֹת תְּמֻתוּן: ⁵ כִּי יֹדֵעַ אֱלֹהִים כִּי בְּיוֹם אֲכָלְכֶם מִמֶּנּוּ וְנִפְקְחוּ עֵינֵיכֶם וִהְיִיתֶם כֵּאלֹהִים יֹדְעֵי טוֹב וָרָע: ⁶ וַתֵּרֶא הָאִשָּׁה כִּי טוֹב הָעֵץ לְמַאֲכָל וְכִי תַאֲוָה־הוּא לָעֵינַיִם וְנֶחְמָד הָעֵץ לְהַשְׂכִּיל וַתִּקַּח מִפִּרְיוֹ וַתֹּאכַל וַתִּתֵּן גַּם־לְאִישָׁהּ

'Ο δὲ ὄφις ἦν φρονιμώτατος πάντων τῶν θηρίων τῶν ἐπὶ τῆς γῆς ὧν ἐποίησε Κύριος ὁ Θεός· καὶ εἶπεν ὁ ὄφις τῇ γυναικί· Τί ὅτι εἶπεν ὁ Θεός, Οὐ μὴ φάγητε ἀπὸ παντὸς ξύλου τοῦ παραδείσου; 2 Καὶ εἶπεν ἡ γυνὴ τῷ ὄφει 'Απὸ καρποῦ τοῦ ξύλου τοῦ παραδείσου φαγούμεθα· 3 'Απὸ δὲ τοῦ καρποῦ τοῦ ξύλου, ὅ ἐστιν ἐν μέσῳ τοῦ παραδείσου, εἶπεν ὁ Θεὸς οὐ φάγεσθε ἀπ' αὐτοῦ, οὐδὲ μὴ ἄψησθε αὐτοῦ, ἵνα μὴ ἀποθάνητε.. 4 Καὶ εἶπεν ὁ ὄφις τῇ γυναικί, Οὐ θανάτῳ ἀποθανεῖσθε· 5 ῟Ηδει γὰρ ὁ Θεὸς, ὅτι ᾗ ἂν ἡμέρᾳ φάγητε ἀπ' αὐτοῦ, διανοιχθήσονται ὑμῶν οἱ ὀφθαλμοί, καὶ ἔσεσθε ὡς Θεοί, γινώσκοντες καλὸν καὶ πονηρόν. 6 Καὶ εἶδεν ἡ γυνὴ ὅτι καλὸν τὸ ξύλον εἰς βρῶσιν, καὶ ὅτι ἀρεστὸν τοῖς ὀφθαλμοῖς ἰδεῖν, καὶ ὡραῖόν ἐστι τοῦ κατανοῆσαι, καὶ λαβοῦσα ἀπὸ τοῦ καρποῦ αὐτοῦ, ἔφαγε·

22

ing that it would lead to wisdom she took the fruit and ate it. And she also offered it to her husband—and he ate it.

[Once that they had eaten] they knew what they had not known, and they knew that they were naked—so they sewed together leaves to make an apron.

עַמָּהּ וַיֹּאכַל : 7 וַתִּפָּקַחְנָה עֵינֵי שְׁנֵיהֶם וַיֵּדְעוּ כִּי עֵירֻמִּם הֵם וַיִּתְפְּרוּ עֲלֵה תְאֵנָה וַיַּעֲשׂוּ לָהֶם חֲגֹרֹת :

καὶ ἔδωκε καὶ τῷ ἀνδρὶ αὑτῆς μετ' αὑτῆς, καὶ ἔφαγον. 7.Καὶ διηνοίχθησαν οἱ ὀφθαλμοὶ τῶν δύο, καὶ ἔγνωσαν ὅτι γυμνοὶ ἦσαν· καὶ ἔρραψαν φύλλα συκῆς, καὶ ἐποίησαν ἑαυτοῖς περιζώματα.

Man did not hesitate here. There is no mention whatsoever that he was reluctant when his wife bid him eat the fruit. He eats it. He does not hesitate. He does not theologize. He does not think. He merely, passively acts—subject to the silent advance of the stronger woman.

Furthermore, man shows that he is without the basic ability to debate. He does not understand the moral issue. It is woman alone who wrestles with the prohibition—and yet the original command not to eat of the fruit of the tree in the middle of the garden came originally to man—not to woman. Still man could not or would not act although it was primarily his responsibility to protect the tree in the center of the garden from any who would touch it or eat of its fruits. Man was a poor watchman. He could not or would not even stop his wife—and she was the only one that he could have stopped since the injuction was only directed to them—if we believe that the first people placed (or created) on earth were Adam and Eve: one man, one woman. Who else could he have guarded the tree from? No one! therefore, at best, the temptation was not directed towards the woman but towards the man to see if he had enough courage and strength of resolve to carry out a divine command. He failed dismally.

He even fails when their "eyes are open" and they discover "their nakedness." Again it is woman who comes to the rescue and sews the aprons. Man is not mentioned.

Even while the aprons are being sewn no where and at no time does man condemn the woman. Instead man blames their tragedy on God—as attested in the use of the verb *ntn*. It is woman who places the blame on the serpent—and it woman's judgement that God accepts:

God said to the woman, "What is the thing that you have done? [to which] the woman replied, "The serpent tricked me, and I ate [the forbidden fruit]."

So God said to the serpent, "Because it was you that did this I will put a special curse on you—greater than on any cattle or any beast of the field, for you shall crawl on your belly and throughout your life you will eat dust."[15]

וַיֹּאמֶר יְהֹוָה אֱלֹהִים לָאִשָּׁה
מַה־זֹּאת עָשִׂית וַתֹּאמֶר הָאִשָּׁה הַנָּחָשׁ
הִשִּׁיאַנִי וָאֹכֵל : וַיֹּאמֶר יְהֹוָה אֱלֹהִים ׀
אֶל־הַנָּחָשׁ כִּי עָשִׂיתָ זֹּאת אָרוּר אַתָּה מִכָּל־
הַבְּהֵמָה וּמִכֹּל חַיַּת הַשָּׂדֶה עַל־גְּחֹנְךָ תֵלֵךְ
וְעָפָר תֹּאכַל כָּל־יְמֵי חַיֶּיךָ :

It is the serpent (or Temptor) that is cursed. Man is not cursed—nor is woman. Man and woman are only *judged* by God.

In the line which most "authorities" read as giving man jurisdiction over woman:

And to woman God said "I will greatly increase your pain and suffering—especially in the experience of giving birth to children; and, you shall also know the pain of desiring your husband..."

. . . . . אֶל־הָאִשָּׁה אָמַר הַרְבָּה
אַרְבֶּה עִצְּבוֹנֵךְ וְהֵרֹנֵךְ בְּעֶצֶב תֵּלְדִי בָנִים
וְאֶל־אִישֵׁךְ תְּשׁוּקָתֵךְ וְהוּא יִמְשָׁל־בָּךְ :

we can only see a sexual reference: to conception and child bearing, and, too, to sexual longing.[16] Even then such "pain" is neither permanent nor scarring. Also this "condemnation" is more directed to the man (*adham*), for man is corrupted by the judgement inasmuch as he is placed in the position of having to administer this pain upon an equal. This "subordination" of woman signifies their shared sin—for from the time of the eating of the forbidden fruit onward, they are "doomed" to experience pain after they have known pleasure.[16]

Furthermore, whereas man and woman had known equality and harmony in creation, in sin the two would know alienation and discord. It is at this point that man names woman *Eve*.[17] By naming woman *Eve*, man asserts his claim over woman.

Man's assertion of claim or authority over woman hardly met with the consent and acceptance of God—for if man's action had been endorsed by God man undoubtedly would have been spared the next punishment. He was not. Instead, after man named woman *Eve* , God expelled man and woman from *Gan Eden*. It is in the expellation of man and woman that we now best see God's attitude. The scriptural passage specifically states that God expelled *adham*: that all important androgynous word for "humankind": man/men *and* woman/women.[18]

God said, "Notice that mankind has become like us [or, 'as one of us'] —by knowing good and evil, for s/he has put forth his/her hand and taken from the tree of life and has eaten it, and shall live [as a species] forever." Therefor God sent mankind from the park called Eden to cultivate the ground from which he evolved.   And thus mankind was driven out at the east end of Eden's garden by agents [who acted for God (literally: Cherubims, or angels)] who held flaming sword(s) to protect the tree of life.

This reference is especially telling. If it is read broadly, as I interpret it, the expellation was of humankind because God feared the rival of now true equals: *"Notice that mankind has become like us..."* This demonstrates the narrow, almost primitive, theological concept of a jealous God who brooked no rival.   Such a conclusion is reenforced in the line *"thus mankind was driven out at the east end of Eden's garden by agents..."* the word *"agents"* is a far more accurate word than "angels" since the agents acted for God rather than independent of God.

Even after the expellation man is not dominate, nor is he independent of woman. On the contrary, man is even-moreso dependent on woman, for woman is necessary for his own physical survival—as well as a compliment to his mental stability. He cannot live alone—a help*mate* is needed to make life easier.[19]

NOTES

1. Exodus 20:17.

2. Exodus 20:12.

3. Genesis 1:26-30.

4. Cf. Deuteronomy 6:4, and Hosea 11:1-11.

5. Hosea 11:9:

6. Genesis 3:21.

7. Nehemiah 9:21 (a function strictly reserved to Israel women).

8. Exodus 17:1-7; Numbers 20:2-13.

9. Exodus 16:4-36; Nehemiah 9:15.

26

10. II Isaiah 42:14, and 66:9; cf, James Muilenburg, "Isaiah 40-66," in *The Interpreters Bible* (New York: Abingdon, 1956) V:473.

11. Genesis 2-3; in reading the first two chapters of Genesis, it should be noted that God compliments each action that is "female" with one that is "male".

12. Genesis 2:23.

13. ‏. . . וְלֹא־אִישׁ בְּחִרְבְּךָ קָדוֹשׁ וְלֹא אָבוֹא בְּעִיר׃‏

14. Genesis 3:16.

15. Genesis 3:14; cf. John A. Bailey, "Initiation and the Primal Woman in Gilgamesh and Genesis 2-3," in the *Journal of Biblical Literature* (June 1970) p. 148.

16. Genesis 3:16.

17. Genesis 3:20. For an interesting perspective, see Else Kahler, *Die Frau in den paulinischen Briefen* (Zurich: Gotthelf-Verlag, 1960) pp. 198-202.

18. Genesis 3:22-24.

19. Cf. Song of Songs 2:10-11, *cum* 3:4.

CHAPTER THREE

WOMAN AFTER EDEN

After the fall of *adham* life remained still on intimate terms of equality. Genesis 3:21 states that both man and woman tailored their clothing together: *"God made man and woman make coats of skins—and clothed them."*

Together they were driven from the park. Together they made their way into a new world and a new life.

Scripture shows, furthermore, that the first truly interpersonal experience was sexual: *"Adam had intercourse with his wife, and she conceived...."*[1]

Sex was certainly a regular part of their life—if we judge the immediacy of the texts, for she soon gave birth yet to another child.[2] However it would be in error to presume that the children were twins, or born close together—instead from this recitation of events we can clearly see that the concept of time was either unimportant, or not well understood—an excellent argument against the Creation theory when it is defined as creation in the span of seven earth-days.

We have no account of what the early days of the two boys were like any more than we have a record of the basic functions of the mothers of all living human-beings (*Eve* translates as "mother of all living"[3])

When one reads the texts following the creation story a more clear picture is available of women and the life of women who lived in ancient Israel: before, during, and after the writing of the Torah—through the days of the authorship of the Torah. Women were, most asuredly, *not* subordinate to men immediately after the Fall in Eden. Early Jewish girls and women were far more free than the Jewess who lived after 200 B.C.E.

For an undetermined period of time—spanning the period from the expellation of *adham*, to the rise of the Law, women in ancient Israel went unveiled at will, moving freely among men. Ancient Israeli women enjoyed (or undertook) a variety of tasks and professions: accepting the work's responsibilities, and benefiting from its rewards.

Many ancient Israeli women tended sheep.[4] Their fields were fertile, their flocks numerous, and their profits certainly were abundant. There is, furthermore, no records of any male interferance in their shepherding methods, nor objections to their talents in watching over the family fortune.

Other ancient Israeli women drew water[5] both for their own personal needs, and for commercial gain. A good portion of the water drawn from wells (and undoubtedly also from streams) was taken to the nearby fields where it was offered (for gratis or profit we do not know) to the multitude of women who gleaned the grains, and harvested the other grasses.[6]

Ancient Israeli women also labored beside men who worked in the field.[7] Those women farmers were neither meek nor mild, nor did they take a backseat to men, with whom they engaged in conversation.[8]

Early Israeli women were not secluded—nor were they excluded from society. They visited, traveled, and enjoyed the company of other women and even other men. Much of the visiting took place in their homes, or in the homes of friends and relatives—but it also transpired along highways, and in the market.[9]

Women greeted strangers, took care of their animals, housed and fed them, and sped them on their way to their final destination. Early Israeli women were, in fact, well known for their hospitality.[10]

Women then, as today, enjoyed fliriting and being

sought out and sought after. At the same time being "too attractive" brought out a protective interest in many men. This protection, however, was not limited strictly to attractive women—a protochivalric interest permeated much of society when any woman was threatened: as was the case of the seven daughters of the priest Midian who had come to the public well to draw water for their father's flock, were driven away by other shepherders (the shepherders' sex is not defined), which aroused the ire of Moses who took it upon himself to defend them.[11]

The change in the status of women, and the diminuation of their rights, came by time of Ramses II (1324-1258 B.C.) and Moses. A good part of the change in attitude and life style came with the increasing difficulties of the time and the unstable political and theological climate.

Israel was a displaced nation. Her people were enslaved. Xenophobia was strong, and the fear of mixing of bloods (Hebrew and foreign) was exceptionally distasteful. To guard against it restrictions were imposed and freedoms severely limited.

When the safeguards did not work, women were reprimanded. As with any community facing a crisis, the nearest element which had become conditioned to a less supportive role was attacked and degraded further so that the active "majority" would take on a false patina of superiority. So, too, it was in this situation. Women became the acused social deviant.

Degenerating the story of Creation to a barbaric tale of the evil of woman who led man into sin, all women were seen as the daughters of "Eve". They were accused of fanning further discontent, taking men away from their labors and prayers, and betraying the quality of the community when they marshalled together, communed openly, or attemted to secure the same social equality that Egyptian women and some other women in the ancient Near East enjoyed. They were now considered the source and cause of all problems, tribulations, and sicknesses.[12]

As the embryonic tale of evil generated by women

evolved into a frightful fantasy of demonic intrigue—including the generation of the tale that women were created before men to bring about the fall of man, restrictions on freedoms multiplied as the throated cries of fearful males pushed against the very heavens that blanketed both sexes. Scorn, fear, and hatred of womankind grew to epidemic proportions. [13]

Womankind was quickly given recognition of having powers tantamount to Lucifer: they could transform and transmorgify at will into either unearthly monsters or unearthly beauties whose sole goal was to ensnare the souls of men which they would engulf as their final testament to their unbridled evil. These souls they would then carnally lay in translation to the very darkness of Sheol.

So complete was the evil prowess of women believed to be that it was recorded that women could even beguile and destroy the very angels of heaven! Even the archangels were powerless before the select denizens of the endless darkness. [14]

When women were not subjecting the heavenly hosts to their mephistophlean charm, it was believed, they determined to torment and bring men down to their unsavory level of licentiousness, sin, and corruption. [15]

Men were to be subjected to the temptations of women, it was believed, so that women could win the riches of the world for themselves. [16] It was commonly believed among men that women were all covetous creatures who unabashedly coveted unceasing erotic and sensual pleasures, fame, and land. To obtain these goals, it was further held, women would use their most sinister and sinful weapon: base carnal instincts leading to the perversion of sex. [17]

With few exceptions sex was viewed negatively. Men believed that sex was a single, solidary, divinely appointed purpose: the procreation of the human species in accordance with the precept "*to be fruitful, go forth, and multiply*".

Furthermore it was believed by many men that the only woman who enjoyed sex was one who was in league with the Devil. A good woman seldom—if ever—thought of sex. She was expected to accept the reality of sex: to see it as the "male right" and her "obligation to endure" it—but never to truly enjoy it—lest she be considered "a fallen woman." Men did not believe women could enjoy sex and still remain a child of God. Her joy, it was argued, was to be in the perpetuation of the chosen people and the fulfillment of the divine commandment.[18]

If woman quietly accepted the sexual attitudes of the male world in which she was forced to be a silent and unassuming part, she was considered to be a "good wife" and praised in the community and in the temple. If she voiced any objections she was damned and could be divorced, put away, or exiled.

If the woman in ancient Israel produced a male offspring to carry on the lineage of his tribe she was considered not only to be an excellent wife but a true daughter of Israel. She could even be called "blessed." But if she failed to produce a male heir she could be divorced or forced like Sara to offer her handmaiden or any other woman to her husband that could give him a son—and then also be compelled to acknowledge the son of the concubine as her own and accord him first place in the house—even if it meant the usurpation of the position of any daughter she may have given birth.[19]

Woman in ancient Israel marked herself blessed by God when she gave birth to her first son. A male heir was a mark of God's favor—and a promise of a blessing to her house and the lineage her body continued. The birth of her son was greeted with rejoicing and celebrations. At that time she was brought to the fore of her friends and relatives and even enjoyed the reverie in public.

The first son never forgot his obligation to his mother for giving him birth. Although he was never commanded by civil or divine law to love her, he was obliged to honor her. He was forbidden to reject her advise,[20] obliged to see to her welfare (as long as she remained a good wife to his father by working diligently and quietly from the break of day to the setting of the sun), and speak well of her.[21]

NOTES

1.   Genesis 4:1.

2.   Genesis 4:2.

3.   Genesis 3:20.

4.   Genesis 3:22-24.

5.   Genesis 24:13; I Samuel 9:11.

6.   Ruth 2:2f.

7.   Genesis 24:15-21, 29:1f; I Samuel 9:11-13.

8.   Ibid..

9.   Genesis 34:1.

10. Genesis 24:13.

11. Exodus 2:16f.

12. I Enoch 19:2; II Enoch 30; Jubilees 3; Testament of
     Reuben 5; Apocalypse of Moses 21:8, 26; Sirac
     25:24f.

13. I Encoh 6:1-72, 16:2-3, 86-89.

14. I Samuel 17.

15. Ibid..

16.   I Kings 21.

17.   *Vitae Adae et Evae* 20:5.3, 35:2-3, 37:2-3.

18.   Genesis 1:22—an injuction actually given to the animals prior to the creation of man. The full text of this injunction reads: *"God created great sea-fish, and every moving creature that lives within the waters, and brought them into existence abundantly according to their individual specie, and so, too, every bird, and let the fowl increase their numbers as well; and, God [then] blessed them and said,* Be fruitful and multiply, and fill the waters of the seas, and let the fowls multiply upon the earth. *And this was accomplished on the fifth day from the morning to the evening."* The second time that this injuction is used is in Genesis 1:28, speaking to the *masters* (a plural noun) of the earth, requiring them, as a people, to be fruitful, take dominion over the earth and the things on and of the earth, and replenish their own number so as to be able to take control over the earth. It is not an injuction to generate progeny for the sake of progenerating progeny.

19.   Genesis 16.   Hagar was finally sent away when Sara's jealousy could no longer tolerate the concubine—although Hagar's exile came only after Sara gave birth herself to a son of Abram. See also Genesis 16:4, 29:31-30:24, and my *Woman, Sex, and Religion*.

20.   Proverbs 9:1-6, 13-18, and 29:3.

21.   Proverbs 1:8, 31:10-31.3.

CHAPTER FOUR

THE WOMAN WITHOUT CHILDREN

A woman who had no son was considered to be a woman without any children.

A childless wife was viewed as a failure: a failure to herself, to her husband, to her community and temple, and to God. A childless wife was seen as one whom God had turned away from.

There was little sympathy for the childless woman. She was greeted with scorn and laughter. Her name was held up to derision. She became the butt for ill-humored jests and teasing.[1]

The family pressures, coupled with the pressures of her society were frequently overwhelming for the childless woman in ancient Israel. In most cases she saw herself as less than a worthy human, and feared the worst. Without a son there was always the promise of a possible divorce, or the forced obligation to secure for her husband a concubine that could give him a son. Even then she was not safe for her dissatisfied husband—who prided himself on his fertility which was equated with divine blessings—could still force her from his house and from the tribe.[2]

Men took inordinate satisfaction in their fecundity. The more sons they generated the more they considered themselves divinely blessed and protected. From Abraham to Jacob there was a near zealousness of divine proportions in the propagations of sons: as Jacob rejoiced in his six sons by Leah—with only a passing remembrance of the daughter

(Dinah).

The recorder of Jacob's geneology then promptly turns to the "opening of Rachel's womb": only to laud it as finding favor with God—demonstrated by the production of the infant male Joseph. Later, when Jacob decides to return to his own land, he takes leave of Laban, and journeys forth with his wives. The next is subtle here, inferring that Rachel was allowed to accompany Jacob since she was the mother of an infant *male*—and, at the same time, hinting that such fortune may not have been her lot if her womb had stayed closed or if she had given birth to a infant *female*.[3]

The story of Jacob and Rachel is, in many way, similar to the earlier account of Abram and Sara. Her lot was also to be initially barren.[4] and of many other women.[5]

Their stories were well known and became the foundation for many social injustices against future generations of barren women, and, too, to the establishment of civil and divine injunctions against celibacy and any sexual act that did not lead to the procreation of future generations. With overpowering eclat such was the support of the injunction formalized in *Kiddushin*:[6]

> *He who reaches the age of twenty and has not married spends all of his days in sin.*

The *Kiddushin* injuction held further that any man or woman who did not marry spent "all of his days in the thought of sin" by contemplating "illicit sex." This illicit sex could range anywhere from the sin of Onan (masturbation to *coitus interruptus*), to premature ejaculation, or even homosexuality.

Homosexuality was, to the majority of the ancient Israelites, frightening since it was considered to be against the divine will—as well as bad for the state which depended upon regular supplies of men to defend its borders and economic interests. Much of this was codified in the

"Holiness Code" of the Book of Leviticus. However, it must be noted, that there are only six passages relating to homosexuality in the Bible—and only one refers to females. From this limitation one can hypothesize that either Israelite males did not conceive of the possibility of lesbianism, or found it to be less offensive than male homosexuality—possibly on the premise that lesbianism was only a "temporary state" for women—one indulged and engaged in when the man was at war or away from the hearth—while male homosexuality was condemned because it appeared to be "effeminate". But even then all six passages do not explicitly and precisely condemn the homosexual act as a deviation of the sexual act itself, but rather condemn the intent and thought of the act: *You must not lie with a man as if he were a woman...* [7]

The statement infers that the objection is against believing that the same result or end will occur when members of the same sex lie together for the purpose of orgasm. The word for the act (or state of activity) is *qadhesh* and as such refers only to the male activity which has unfortunately been regularly translated either as "sodomy" or "sodomite" in reflection on the city of Sodom. In truth the word refers to any form of male-male sexual activity—which few women could perform even given suggestive apparatus. The impact is upon the action or practice—not the condition or state of mind. Therefore the actual condemnation is the deliberate and conscious attempt of a heterosexual to engage in sexual activity with another member of the same sex rather than participating with a member of the opposite sex, while at the same time acting towards the partner of the same sex as if s/he were the opposite sex. Few true homosexuals, then or today, engage in a sexual activity believing his/her partner to be a member of the opposite sex. Even here there is no injunction against lesbianism—nor is there any explicit condemnation against lesbianism anywhere throughout Old or New Testaments—including often quoted, badly interpreted passage in Romans 1:26f.

To avoid the stigma of being given "to selfish vices" or contemplating "illicit sex," many women married whomever was available. Marriages were arranged; love had little to do with most marriages, and love in a marriage is seldom expressed in scripture.

Marriage was important. The Law and the interpretations of the law emphasized the importance of marriage, arguing: *a man without a wife is not called a man, as it is written "Male and female He created them, and He called their name Adam."*[8]

To reject any acceptable offer of marriage was to reject the social order and endanger the state. To reject the social order and endanger the state was tantamount to separating oneself from one's past, present, and future—and frequently even severing the ties of kith and kin.

At the same time marriages were not to be contracted hastily. To enter into a marriage hastily was considered to be as inane as to enter into a marriage because of a reason of the heart. The *Talmud* ruled that the best marriages were those marriages which were fruitful—where children were born regularly and plentifully, and where both husband and wife worked at the marriage. To achieve this marriage it was believed that only the eldest male relative could suitably contract a spouse for the kin of marriageable age. "Marriagable age" usually came immediately after puberty for the girl, and near the late teens for the boy. It could come as early as 10, however, but this tender age was usually reserved to be the lot of the female.[9]

When a child was considered to be of marriagable age the senior male member of the family contacted his nearest kin removed from the degrees of consanguinity. The future spouse was usually chosen from within the same tribe.[10]

Once that the marriage had been determined and agreed upon, the contract was written. Rarely, at best, was either the bride or the groom permitted to see the contract (or reject it!)[11]

After the contract had been agreed upon, the

raison d'etre for the marriage was spelled out. Paramount among the inclusions was the injunction for the woman to spend her married life "grinding corn, suckling children, being a beautiful wife, and having numerous children."[12]

The *cause célèbre* occured when the future bride was offered a present. This "bride piece" was usually only of nominal value. Most commonly it was but a single *denari*: one penny.

Once that the bride piece was presented and accepted, a public declaration of the betrothal was made. Following the declaration a formal document, of some nature, was drawn up and witnessed.

There was no marriage ceremony, as is known in the twentieth century, between the two. The marriage was considered made, finalized, and divinely consecrated, when the man and woman successfully completed sexual intercourse.[13]

Sexual union was required. Not only was the sexual coupling imperative for the society to accept the act of marriage as having taken place, but more significant was the all important discovery of whether or not the bride was a biological virgin. If there had been any doubt of the woman's virginity—as testified by the existence of "the blood sheet" consecrated by the splitting of the hymen—the man (be it groom, or any other male member of the groom's family) could compel the woman to "prove" her virginity by taking an oath or having testators testify to her never "having known a man before". Such a requirement, however, was never demanded of the man who was immune to any social demand of his being "chaste".[14]

If the bride could not prove her virginity, she could be ceremoniously stoned to death—unless she publicly pleaded rape.[15] The death penalty was mandatory, for it was believed that a woman who gave her virginity to anyone other than her own husband had committed a "crime against Israel" and against her family—equal to theft and treason.[16]

If she was able to prove that she was a virgin, or was acquitted for the crime of not being a virgin by successfully proving rape, she was allowed to enter into the marriage state.

Originally all Israelite marriages were monogamous.[17] This changed quickly, however, and polygamy was the order of the day from Lamech having his two wives (as did Jacob), "to comfort him"[18], to Solomon's harem.[19]

Polygamy in ancient Israel was of course discriminatory. While men could have more than one wife, women were forbidden to have more than one husband at any one time.

Discrimination against women went further. A husband was allowed to be jealous, accuse his wife of all manner of improprieties, abuse her, and require her to undertake a cultic test to determine whether or not she had been faithful, just, or "wifely" in her duties and responsibilities to him and his house.[20] At the same time no similar recourse was offered to the woman who felt that she was left out by a man who accepted little if any responsibility.[21]

Women in ancient Israel were to cater to men in all things and at all times. And, although it was considered unseemly, and even at times sinful for the wife to seek, desire, or enjoy sex, *Ketubot* admonishes the woman of Israel to give her husband as much sex as he was demanding and she was capable of—so that he would not be "compelled, and forced into sin" by having to go outside of the marriage to "meet his needs" and passion for sex. If the husband "did stray beyond the bonds of marriage" it was considered to be solely the wife's fault: a man was not capable of straying and sining sexually as long as his wife fulfilled his "needs" and "longings."[22] In this regard it must be noted that it is woman, and not man, who is the "instigator" of sex—woman alone is considered to be the siren of sex. If she employed sex outside of marriage it was considered a sin ("prostitution), but if she used it within marriage for the overt purpose of procreation, it was"rightful and a blessing."

Women had only one token of justice in this barbaric code of "holiness". If a husband avoided his wife—even under the excuse of studying the Torah, or engaging in too long a prayer, or giving too much time to charity, or other such excuses—the husband was at fault, and such avoidance could cost him the favor of God. If man forfeited the favor of God because he "stayed away from his wife" he could be killed by that same God—and, it was believed, such was usually the case if the husband found another avenue for his sexual release when his wife was available and willing to meet "his needs."[23]

As long as both the husband and the wife were able, capable, and willing to have sex with one another, they were expected to do so regularly—or face "the wrath of God". The only exception to this injction was in case of war when the man was excused from "fulfilling his marriage obligation and right."

In cases of war man was expected to totally abstain from all forms of sex. He was not to have intercourse with his wife, masturbate, or engage in any homosexual encounter, for it was believed that sex during war was detrimental to the man's total health: mental as well as physical. It was commonly held that sex drained all strength from the body of a man, thus making him incapable of bearing arms and prosecuting combat and defense; it was, furthermore, even believed that sex was so overtaxing that a man temporarily lost his ability to function in all other regards as a man—the only solution being to rest after the sexual act, then purify himself, pray, and resolve to work harder. This idea became so impregnated in the ancient (and succeeding) society that the unhealthy phobia developed around the physical emission itself, because of the belief that sexual intercourse which came to its climax drained the blood strength from the man directly into the woman, and thus gave the woman the opportunity and ability to best the man in a fight—and win! with the consequence that the woman would rule over the man.[24]

Out of inordinate fear of being controlled by a woman, ancient Israelite men were willing to abstain from sex unless they felt assured that such an act would lead to procreation—especially of future males. The full spectra of childbearing became a paradox: sex was sinful and harmful (to the male), yet it was necessary to "be fruitful and multiply." Furthermore: the conception and birth of a boy-child was a blessing for it proved the man to have been in the favor of God who directed the strength of the seminal emission into the full creation of a manchild; while the conception and birth of a girl-child was seen as a quasi-alienation of God and man, for it was held that man had not won total favor with God—a God who then punished man by directing the seminal emission into "imperfect channels" which led to the "part-birth of man": the creation of a womanchild, who could neither defend Israel nor win the full favor of the Israelite God.

The concern of the sex of the unborn therefore led the ancient Israelite society into a full cycle of emotions and strategies. The sexual act was unclean but necessary; the impregnated woman was bearing the punishment of *Eve* who had been cursed with the pain of childbearing, yet while she was pregnant she was not plagued with "the discharge of blood"; and, finally, in the act of childbirth (a state which was universally lamented!), she became unclean again for "blood issued forth" in the birthing act itself which was frequently considered tantamount to leprosy or being in contact with a corpse—or at least socializing with any of the "unclean".[25]

The only aspect considered good relevant to child-birth, was the male attitude of winning a prophetic sign. Woman's suffering (from childbirth of a living heir, or the birthing of one stillborn, to the experiencing of death of the heir after birth) was believed to be the promise of Israel's future days. Israel was a woman who would also have to undergo the travail for the sins of her people; God would listen to her cries, and comfort her by new generations which would determine her destiny.[26] Only after woman (and Israel) gave birth, became purified through ritual and prayer, would woman (and Israel) find peace. And Israel, like mortal woman, was prone to render herself unclean again through the "flowing of blood": woman through her menstrual cycle, and Israel through war, murder, and similar crimes that led to the flow of blood.

So terrified of the "flow of blood" did the society become that any one who "let blood" was banned from any direct social or religious intercourse with the rest of the society. For that reason the woman, like the murderer or warrior, was forbidden to teach or prophecize: she could neither be priest nor rabbis, and the services that she may have wished to render to her community were forbidden. She was considered "unclean" and everything she touched was "unclean"—thereby to allow her near the Holy of Holies or the Sacred Scrolls was to allow Israel to be defiled and invite the vengeance of God who would bring to Israel a mortal holocaust.

NOTES

1.   Genesis 16:1-2, 30:1-3; I Samuel 1:2; Judges 11:1-3.

2.   Genesis 30:1-2, 22-23; Leviticus 12:2, 5.

3.   Genesis 29.

4.   Genesis 30:1-2   יַתֵּרֶא רָחֵל כִּי לֹא יָלְדָה לְיַעֲקֹב
וַתְּקַנֵּא רָחֵל בַּאֲחֹתָהּ וַתֹּאמֶר אֶל־יַעֲקֹב
הָבָה־לִּי בָנִים וְאִם־אַיִן מֵתָה אָנֹכִי :
וַיִּחַר־אַף יַעֲקֹב בְּרָחֵל וַיֹּאמֶר הֲתַחַת
אֱלֹהִים אָנֹכִי אֲשֶׁר־מָנַע מִמֵּךְ פְּרִי־בָטֶן :
cp. Genesis 16:1-2.

5.   Genesis 20:18, 22-23, 30:26; I Samuel 1:3-7, 11; II Samuel 6:20-23; Judges 11:1-3.

6.   *Kiddushin* 29b.

7.   Romans 1:27.

8.   Genesis 1:27, as cited in *Yevamot* 36a; cp. Leviticus

12:2, 5.

9. *Kiddushin* 12.

10. Genesis 24; 34:1-4. Judges 14:12.

11. Genesis 24:5, 57-58.

12. *Ketubot* 56b.

13. *Kiddushin* 2a.

14. Deuteronomy 22:13-21.

15. Deuteronomy 22:21f.

16. Ibid.

17. Genesis 2:21-24; 7:7 וַיַּפֵּל יְהֹוָה אֱלֹהִים תַּרְדֵּמָה עַל־הָאָדָם

18. Genesis 4:19.

19. I Kings 11:1-3.

20. Numbers 5:14, 31.

21. Numbers 5:11-31.

22. *Ketubot* 65a.

23. Cf. I Kings 1:1-4; Judges 5:28-30, 19:22-24; cp. Deuteronomy 21:10-14; on the joy of sex, see *Song of Songs*, and Hosea 2:14-15.

24. Proverbs 31:3; cp. *Ketubot* 62b.

25. Leviticus 12-15.

26.   Leviticus is emphatic on the exclusion of women from the priesthood; see, Leviticus 15:19-33: notice the prohibition based on the menstruation cycle—and the "blessing" men have since they do not menstruate which permits them to be priests.

Malachi is even more emphatic. Men alone, he argues are "clean" while all women, due to their mentsrual cycle are permanently "unclean". Since men alone are "clean" they have been especially chosen by God to be the priests of God and handle all of the rituals and duties first given to Aaron—who was a man. See Malachi 2:7-8; cp. Leviticus 10:10, and, Numbers 18:5.

The Wailing Wall — Jerusalem

After 70 A.D. this wall became a scene of religious fervor among the Jews, who stood before it and bewailed the Roman destruction of the Temple. It is the only remaining part of the foundation of the Temple Mount begun by Solomon and extended by Herod in the first century B.C.E.

Palestine in the 9th Century B.C.

CHAPTER FIVE

WOMAN AS VIEWED BY THE TALMUD

Women have little place in the Talmud—or in Talmud society. The have no rights and even fewer opportunitites.

Women have no obligation to teach themselves, under the Talmud. Nor are they obligated to teach other women. They are strictly forbidden to teach men.

According to the Talmud, women have but one single merit. This merit was expressed most graphically by Rabbi Hiya, who decreed: [1]

> *Their* [woman's] *merit arises from the fact that they take their children to their places of study and that they receive their husbands when they* [the husbands] *return home.*

The only positive requirements were that women were to keep their family pure (*niddah*), to separate the dough necessary to the preparation of the loaves of bread (*hallah*), and to light the Sabbath candles.

The Talmud further states that woman's dignity came only with marriage: [2]

> *A woman is* golem: *a shapeless lump, and concludes a covenant of marriage only with him who transforms her into a finished vessel.*

and, again: [3]

> *The Divine Presence rests only upon a married man because an unmarried man is but half a man. The Divine Presence does not rest upon that which is imperfect* [which is woman].

Woman was imperfect because of the fantasy of Lilith. Lilith was a female demon in Jewish demonology. She had a central role in all evil.

The fantasy of Lilith can be traced back to Babylonian lore. Some account of this female monster even has antecedents in ancient Sumeria. The Babylonians called her Lilu. Sumerians named her Lilitu. However in both cases, etymologically neither Lilu or Lilitu comes near the Hebrew Lilith (or *laylah*) which stands for night. Still each carries similar properties and attributes, for all are *mazikim* (or "harmful spirits"). Some attack and harm males—sexually, mentally, and/or physically, while others endanger women in childbirth and the child immediately following birth.

In most cases these monsters are winged creatures—like gargoyles. Isaiah argued that these creatures would lay waste the lands of the earth on the Final Day.[4]

Midrashic literature expands the importance and role of Lilith. According to this material Lilith was Adam's second wife—after Eve died. In this literature, Lilith is not the name of the second wife, but a term expressing the properties of the woman who is given the name Piznai.

The account in the tale is simple. Piznai has sex frequently with Adam, and gives birth to a host of male and female demons.[5] These off-spring are so numerous that they fill the world that it became customary to write amulets against these later progeny of First Man. Here sex and sexuality form a major part of the testament. The evil of their sexual life together came with enjoyment of the physical act which led the Lilith to arguing with Adam over the manner of their intercourse. Lilith did not wish to be submissive at all times. She sought equality even in sexuality.

When Adam would not agree to sexual equality Lilith left. Adam became so upset over her leaving that he talked God into sending angels after her—angels with the most unique names: Snwy, Snsnwy, and Smnglf.

God's angels found Lilith in the Red Sea. They ordered

18th century Persian amulet worn for the protection of the new-born child against Lilith. Adam's second wife, Lilith, is represented with outstretched arms and is bound in fetters. On her body is written, "Protect this newborn child from all harm," and on either side of her are inscribed the names of Adam and Eve, and the patriarchs and matriarchs, while above her are the initial letters of a passage from Numbers 6:22-27 (*...bless the children of Israel and say to them, the Lord shall bless and protect you...*), and below are the initial letters from Psalm 121. The amulet measures 9.1x6.7 cm. (3½x2½ in.), and is in the Feuchtwanger Collection in the Israel Museum, Jerusalem, donated by Baruch and Ruth Rappaport.

her to return to Adam or witness 100 of her sons die every day she stayed away from Adam's bed.

Lilith refused. It was her purpose, she claimed, to harm newborn infants, even if those infants were her own.

The angels accepted Lilith's arguments reluctantly, for she, like the first Eve, was intelligent and rational and argued with conviction. Still they were able to extract from Lilith the promise never to harm a child which wore an amulet which carried the image of an angel.[6]

To avoid the pitfalls of a Lilith ancient Israelite women were warned to remain dutiful, obedient, and faithful to their husbands. She was only valuable to the society, therefore, when she married. Her completeness came only with the propagation of the tribe—provided that the newborn lived, escaping the dangers of Lilith.

To protect herself the Israelite wife took the name of her

husband—discarding her own. She listened and obeyed every word he uttered—sought him out for advice on all matters—seeing in him the earthly representative of God. She ignored her own individuality, needs, and interests—convincing herself that his desires and needs were her own. Her joy was in her home (*d'baita*) as it was initimately equated with her function as wife (as seen so graphically in the Aramaic language of the Talmud which uses the word *d'baita* for both "wife" and "home").[7]

Public life was severely restricted with the advance of Israelite society. After the cities developed her sole public exposure and experience came when she fetched water from the common well, or gathered victuals and other essentials.

When woman did appear in public she was to go veiled—and avoid the glances of men.[8] Her conversation was limited as were her associations for fear that passerbys would view her as a prostitute.

Her life and actions were governed by the Torah and the Talmud. She had little freedom.

Ancient Israeli laws were emphatically anti-woman. She was evil and the instigator of all wrong doings. She was the instrument of crime and sin.[9]

Woman alone could betray society.[10] The betrayal was brought on by a look, glance, or even the tenor of her voice which was considered so sexually seductive that even an orthodox Jew could be led into straying from his prayers if she was allowed near the temple.[11] For that reason woman was forbidden to speak in the synagogue.[12]

Women who appeared near the synagogue or temple were labeled prostitutes—for a prostitute "won her victims" by the "smoothness of her tongue" which was treacherous and loose—and which would lead even the most pious into impiety.[13]

The Book of Proverbs details that women not only are given to veiled speech and evil conversations, but that they are noisy and distracting to pious men—wantonly basking in contentiousness and conivings.[14] Still they are also described as weak, cowardly, and afraid.[15] If a woman was found to be composed of all of these elements she was *ipso facto* also guilty of prostitution and treason.

Prostitution was defined broadly. It was more than sex for payment.

Prostitution was any act or word which led man away

from clean thoughts, words, or deeds.

There was one paradox—common in any chauvinistic civilization: prostitution was a profession accorded to only one of the sexes—in this case women. Ancient Israelites had a difficult time reconciling—and admitting—that prostitution also flourished among men who sold their sexual favors to women and even other men.

A female prostitute was any womn who had sex willingly with any man prior to marriage—even if the man she had sex with was her fiance; the crime itself was considered to have been comitted when "she did not cry for help" if it was done in the city.[16] Any woman caught "playing the role of a harlot" was to be burned.[17] The man, on the other hand—like Judah, the son of Jacob, was not attacked nor his goods or wealth attached.[18]

At the same time various records, including the various books of the Old Testament, testify to the reality that temple prostitution flourished.[19] Concubines were sold for the basic purpose of sex[20] and few restraints were placed upon the man and his sexual urges.

Men, on the other side of the coin, were damned not as prostitutes, but as homosexuals if they lay with men in the pretense of being a woman (*mishk^ebhey ishshah*—literally: "the lyings of a woman")[21] Here the condemnation is not over the overt act but the covert intent: the act of homosexual sexual expression is damned only because the man "lowered" himself to the status of *acting* as if he were a woman (as seen in the Septuagint which has *koiten gunaikos*, which the Vulgate has translated as *coitu femineo*). It was condemned because it was closely associated with pagan civilizations which were considered idolatrous—as was seen with the Egyptians who were matriarchal and matrilineal in familial considerations.[22]

While the Law was emphatic on the point discussed above, rabbinical thought was more mild. *Mishnah* condemned homosexuality in force and prostitution in part only if the act was a "wanton transgression". Women were almost always condemned, however, for women were "inherently" wanton.[23]

Yet while priests and prophets denounced all forms of prostitution, prostitution existed—and flourished. Even those who denounced it most bitterly were frequently its regular participants—and some, such as Hosea, married the "common whore," although, it must be noted, they excused themselves and their marriages on the ground that such acts were charitable—their intent being to convert the prostitute from a life of sin and debauchery.

The case of Hosea is worth reviewing. A flashing eyed religious fanatic, he fell in love with a beautiful pagan prostitute. He married her—hoping and praying for her conversion to the One God of Israel. She did not. Nor did she give up her profession—for she thoroughly enjoyed her work.

Disgusted with his wife's open "sinfulness" Hosea sold her into slavery—with near religious zeal under the premise that if you can not convert your opponent—destroy that opponent!

Hosea's sale of his wife was legal—according to the Mosaic Law. However he did not find a great deal of satisfaction in his action. He soon discovered that he missed his wife and even loved her—all the time realizing that such an attitude and psychology was dangerous since it was displeasing to the God of Israel.

Risking the wrath of God Hosea bought back his wife and took her to his home. Not assured that this was safe he carried off into the desert and attempted to woo her all over again! (most of his contemporaries would have left their wife-prostitutes in slavery! feeling that it would have not only been most pleasing to God, but also less difficult!). Hosea, however, was not of the same persuasion as his peers. Hosea believed God hated divorce[24] even as much as God hated "indecency"[25] (which included everything from burning the day's bread to adultery!). Therefore Hosea kept his wayward woman!

Divorce was a facet of life in ancient Israel—one facet not quibbled over by many who did not have the resolve of Hosea. While "indency" was a general charge, the actual charge had to be stronger. By the time of the Talmud divorce was relegated to two grounds only: if a husband accused his wife falsely of "unchastity" or if he raped a virgin (the later requiring him to marry the "offended" woman) .

Obtaining a divorce was difficult as time evolved. To avoid the loss of time and face men generally preferred to either secure concubines or control more rigidly their wives.

To keep a wife faithful the majority of men in ancient Israel became authoritarian. Strict adherence to the Law was the rule. If the senior male member of a household had to leave on business or to visit the Temple, the next eldest male was placed in charge over the house and the women of the house. To govern the women and "keep them from evil" tasks were rigorously assigned: from drawing water, to cleaning, sweeping, gathering wood and chips, gleaning and grinding, shearing and reaping, if the women were confined to the house.

NOTES

1. Leviticus 15:19-33.

2. *Sanhedrin* 22b.

3. *Zohar Hadash* 4, 506.

4. Isaiah 34:14.

5. Midrash in *Ha-Goren*, 9 (1914) 66-68.

6. *Ba-Midbar Rabbah*, end of chapter 16. See A.M. Killen's article in *Revue de littérature comparée* 12 (1932), 277-311.

7. Shabbat 118b; see my *Woman in Biblical Israel*, p. 23.

8. Joachim Jeremias, *Jerusalem in the times of Jesus,* in *loc. cit.*, pp. 360-365.

9. Cf. *Tosebtra Brahot* 7.18. Cp. Leviticus 27:2-8.

10. M. Noth, *The Laws in the Pentateuch & Other Studies* (Philadelphia: Fortress Press, 1966) pp. 55f. Cp. Proverbs 2:16, 5:3, 9:13, 11:22; Deuteronomy

11. *Berahot* 24a.

12. *Megillah* 23a.

13. Proverbs 2:16, 5:3, 6:26.

14. Proverbs 9:13, 21:9, 19, 25:24.

15. Isaiah 19:16; cf. Jeremiah 50:37, 51:30.

16. Deuteronomy 22:23.

17. Leviticus 21:9.

18. Genesis 38:12-19.

19. II Kings 23:7.

20. Exodus 21:7-11.

21. Leviticus 18:22.

22. See my *Woman in the ancient Near East,* pp. 70-92.

23. See E. Westermarck, *Early Beliefs and their Social Influence* (London, 1908) p. 129.

24. Malachi 2:15f.

25. Deuteronomy 24:1f. Cf. Deuteronomy 22:13-19, 28. For the Talmud grounds for divorce, requiring a special document to be drawn up detailing specific reasons why the divorce was sought, see *Gitten* 26a.

CHAPTER SIX

WOMEN AND WORK IN ANCIENT ISRAEL

Not all women in ancient Israel stayed home—nor did they stay indoors. And not all women were under male domination and control.

Some women in ancient Israel served as servants. Others were cooks or bakers—working either for wealthy Israelites or in commercial enterprise serving the general public.

Records detail the trade of women who created and sold perfume.[1] We read of several highly competent and successful nurses,[2] and there were even a few celebrated midwives and physicians who were women.[3]

It was not uncommon to find women in ancient Israel who made their living as professional mourners, while still others were trained undertakers and embalmers; some even made their living as grave diggers.[4]

While men in general, and rabbis in particular viewed all women as being "lightheaded" or "without any intelligence at all", there exist many records of women highly learned and competent who in their own day disproved the general myth of women's intelligence being inferior to the male intelligence. The most graphic account comes from the *Sanhedrin*:[5]

> *The emperor once said to Rabban Gamaliel:*
> *Your God is a thief, for it is written:* And the Lord
> God caused a deep sleep to fall upon the man [*Adam*]
> and he slept [*and took one of his ribs, etc...*]. ...
> *Thereupon his* [the emperor's] *daughter said*
> *to him: leave him to me and I will answer him, and*
> [turning to the emperor] *said; Give to me a com-*

mander!

Why do you need him? asked he.

[The emperor's daughter responded] *Thieves broke in last night and robbed us of a silver pitcher— leaving a golden one in its place.*

I wish that we would receive such visits every night, he exclaimed.

Ah! she retorted; was it not to Adam's benefit that he was deprived of a rib and received a wife to serve him?

Although chauvinistic in tone and story, this account reveals a great deal to the reader. Not only does woman show her capability to reason—but to reason beyond the scope and power of many men. Furthermore, this account shows at least one woman's realization that man can function better with the assistance of woman. The passage "and receive a wife to serve him" might be better understood as a compliment than an insult to womankind—the author undoubtedly carried the inane idea that women in general were placed on this earth to be slaves to me—a common idea at the time of the recording of the story—however it also gives support to the reality that the sexes need one another. The same thesis can be seen in other accounts which traditionally downplay the role of women, or worse yet, argue that women are traditionally evil and coniving. Thus in a new perspective one can see the ambition and earnestness of Jezebel who wished only for her husband's (Ahab) advancement—which is scripturally condemned, but certainly in line with contemporary Machiavellian philosophy of "the end justifies the means." Jezebel could be any ambitious woman who is serious about her economic situation and station and desires only the best for her husband and family. Contemporary economic reality would praise her— not damn her![6]

Even the story of David and Bathsheba can be viewed in a contemporary light. Although it is a story of adultery—

it was not the adultery of Bathsheba—but the adultery of
David. Her bathing style and location was not unusual.
Public bathing historically has been common. It was David
who lusted after Bathsheba—not Bathsheba who desired
David. His treachery was far greater than hers—for it was he
who sent her husband to the front—without consulting her
or taking into consideration her desires. His sexuality was
forced upon her—it was tanatamount to rape! and yet he is
praised and his abuse ignored.[7]

The treachery of men in scripture is generally ignored
or overlooked. This double standard is especially acute in
the tale of Sampson and Delilah. If Delilah had worked for
the Israelites instead of the Philistines she would have been
praised as a heroine. Instead she is damned as a traitor—yet
the act of fornication on the part of Sampson is singularly
underplayed and he is held up as a martyr! His placing his
head in her lap is recorded without mention—and the more
than probable sexual exchange is ignored—both acts which
theologically are condemned for the plethora of sexual expression and techniques is not permitted in the Law of the
Old Testament.

Yet while the apparent evils of select women (such as
Delilah) are recounted gleefully in the Old Testament, there
is only cursory mention of the saviorship of women who
significantly contributed to Israelite history and posterity.
How little is said about the valiant Deborah who in earnest
love to save Israel slew the mighty and hated Siseri:[8]

תְּבֹרַךְ מִנָּשִׁים יָעֵל אֵשֶׁת חֶבֶר הַקֵּינִי
מִנָּשִׁים בָּאֹהֶל תְּבֹרָךְ ‬ יָמַיִם שָׁאַל חָלָב
נְבְגָה בְּסֵפֶל אַדִּירִים הִקְרִיבָה חֶמְאָה :

Then, too, there is the account of the valorous Miriam who
cunningly protected the infant Moses from the Egyptians
army which sought to slay all male infant Israelites. Her
only goal being to give Israel as savior who could free her
people, eventhough the courageous act she undertook could
have cost her her own life.[9]   And, then, too, there is the

all important story of the Queen of Sheba who came to Solomon, bringing gifts to Israel, and elected to stay and exchange confidences. In fact the record clearly and specifically states "there was nothing that the king hid from her which he did not tell her"—a mark of favor and trust usually reserved for men—but in this case accorded to a woman. She was his equal.[10]

Whether or not the Queen of Sheba was a living human being (which I discuss in my book *Woman in the World of Ancient Arabia*) is not important at this time. What is significant is that the scriptures give recognition to a woman who could be trusted with knowledge of state importance. At the same time the records of the Kings of Israel acknowledge Solomon's great promiscuity—he had no less than 700 wives, 300 concubines, and unnumbered mistresses. God was not angry because of his promiscuity—God only becomes angry when his wives lead him into serving "strange" gods (Ashtoreth, Milcom, Chemosh, and Molech) and building them temples.[11]

NOTES

1. I Samuel 8:13.

2. Genesis 24:59, 35:8; Exodus 2:7; II Samuel 4:4; II Kings 11:2; II Chronicles 22:11; Ruth 4:6.

3. Genesis 35:17, 38:28; Exodus 1:15-21.

4. Jeremiah 9:17.

5 *Brahot* 10a; cp. *Ketubot* 65a, *Sanhedrin* 39a; cf. *Kiddushin* 80b, which ridicules women as being "lightheaded", cp. Esther 1:20 and Judith 16:6-7, for a Biblical response to this charge.

6. I Kings 21.

7. II Samuel 11.

8. Judges 5:24-26, and

יָדָהּ לַיָּתֵד תִּשְׁלַחְנָה וִימִינָהּ לְהַלְמוּת עֲמֵלִים וְהָלְמָה
סִיסְרָא מָחֲקָה רֹאשׁוֹ וּמָחֲצָה וְחָלְפָה רַקָּתוֹ:

9. Exodus 2:1-4. See how she is listed as one of the
main sources of Israelite freedom in Micah 6:4, a
passage often forgotten or overlooked.

10. I Kings 10:1-2.

11. II Kings 11:5-9.

כָּל־יֹשְׁבֵי תֵבֵל וְשֹׁכְנֵי אָרֶץ כִּנְשֹׁא־נֵס
הָרִים תִּרְאוּ וְכִתְקֹעַ שׁוֹפָר תִּשְׁמָעוּ:

CHAPTER SEVEN

ADULTERY: THE DOUBLE STANDARD

By legal and religious definition adultery was a crime committed primarily by women whose victims were men. The man was guilty of being led by a woman into "sin"— while the woman was guilty of betraying the basic purity of the man.

Adultery was also a crime. It was tantamount to murder and theft. Adultery was considered to be the murder of the marriage and the theft of a man's property.

There was but one punishment considered suitable to fit the crime of adultery. The punishment was to be stoned until dead.[1]

There was some question as to the nature, extent and reason for adultery in the trial of an adulteress or adulterer if that "criminal" was not caught in the act of committing the "crime." The marginal difference appeared in how the parties involved in the adultery were viewed by the court. While both the man and the woman could be damned to the same penalty:[2]

וַיֹּאמֶר דָּוִד אֶל־אוּרִיָּה שֵׁב בָּזֶה גַּם־
הַיּוֹם וּמָחָר אֲשַׁלְּחֶךָּ וַיֵּשֶׁב אוּרִיָּה
בִירוּשָׁלַםִ בַּיּוֹם הַהוּא וּמִמָּחֳרָת:

the man was somewhat excused on the grounds that he had "sinned", while the woman was unceremoniously proclaimed a common harlot.[3]

Judging adultery was unique. Any couple caught in the act of adultery were immediately condemned and publicly stoned.

If the act was only suspected but no proof was available, the "offended" husband could require his wife to stand trial. Her trial was a religio-juridico ordeal—in many ways a forerunner to the Trials by Ordeal of the European Middle Ages. In both cases the outcome (or verdict) rested upon divine whim (or intercession or interference!) The Book of Numbers spells it out rigorously:[4]

> ...*And God said to Moses:* Speak to the children of Israel and say to them, *if the wife of any man should stray and commit a transgression against him by having sex with a man other than her husband, and she keep this transgression hidden from her husband because she has done the act without his knowledge; and if there were no witnesses who saw her commit this sin, and she has not been found out, still the husband will become jealous and be afraid that his wife has slept with another man; then that man shall bring his wife to the priest and he shall give an offering for her which will be one tenth of an* ephah *of barley meal—just it—and he shall pour no oil upon it, nor shall he put any frankincense upon it: for it is a meat-offering of jealousy, a memorial meat-offering bringing the memory of the iniquity to mind. And the priest shall bring the accused wife near, and shall place her before the Lord. And the priest shall take sanctified water in an earthen vessel, and also some dust that is on the floor of the tabernacle, and he shall take it into his hand, and he shall put it into the water. Then the priest shall put the woman before the presence of God, and he will uncover the head of the woman and put on her hands the meat-offering of memorial for it is a meat-offering of jealousy. In the hands of the priest shall be the bitter waters that bring the curse.*

And the priest shall charge her by requiring an oath. He shall say to the woman: If no man has had sex with you, and if you have not gone out on your husband, then you are free from the bitterness of this water which shall be your judge. But if you have left your husband [*for another man*], and if you have been defiled [*by the other man*] and you have had sex with a man other than your husband: *then the priest shall charge and curse the woman with an oath, of imprecation, and say to that woman* the Lord will curse you and your people and will cause your thigh to fall off, and your belly will swell up! and the water that shall cause this curse to come true will go into your bowels and make your belly swell [*even further*] and then your legs will rot. [*Therefore woman*] you shall say Amen. Amen. [It shall be so, it shall be so].

If her belly did not swell, nor her leg rot and fall off she was judged innocent. But, usually before she took the water, fearing the unknown and worried that the water might make her belly swell and her leg fall off, the woman confessed whatever the men wished to hear—even to incriminating herself for an act for which she was not responsbible nor committed. She lived in an age of superstition that hid behind a cloak of religion, and the word of a priest was believed to be the word of God.

Some women did survive the mental anguish of the ordeal. Most were "proven" innocent. Those who were proven innocent were allowed to return to their homes and hearths. The community basically forgave them, and at times celebrated their exoneration. Her husband suffered no penalty for his false accusation. The wife had no recourse against her husband's unfair accusation. She could neither sue nor demand a private or public apology.. She was *ishshah* which had become corrupted to mean "belonging to a man"!

To discourage further accusations and to escape any abuse (physical or otherwise) the woman frequently surrendered everything including her dignity and freedom of individuality and self determination as to what was right or wrong. She was praised as being discreet, loyal, and silent—anything but *adham*: an equal.[5]

If the woman was not silent she could be punished both by God and by man. Her silence was to be complete—she was neither to question nor rebuke. Man's choices were to be accepted tacitly. No matter what man did woman was forbidden to demur, question, or object—or her lot would be the same misfortune as Miriam who had spoken against Moses' choice of wives, for which she was struck with leprosy![6] If her crime was not exceptionally grevious—one which would require divine vengance—the woman could still face a fate that was considered equal to death—she could be divorced!

Divorce was strictly, and totally, the right and prerogative of the man. It was simple for the man, for all the man had to do was to write out a bill of divorce, give it to his wife, and order her to leave his house. He could determine the divorce necessary regardless of the reason at whim, for he himself was the sole judge on the validity and value of their union. She had no say, no rights, no recourse. The Law expressed his omnipotence succinctly: *If then she finds no favor in his eyes because he has found some indecency in her, then let him write her a bill of divorcement, and place it into her hand, and send her out of his house.*[7]

There was no provision for the wife of an equal nature. If she lived with a cruel husband, a drunkard, or a thief, she had to endure her existence—even if living with such a man threatened her life and health—save for one rare exception. The exception came in the area of sex.

A woman was expected to give her husband an heir—a male issue. If her husband died without giving "her seed" that lived, his brother was expected to marry the widow and make her pregnant. If the brother refused to marry his brother's widow, or to have sex with her which lead to the creation of a child, the wife was permitted to go to the city fathers (elders) and proclaim that her dead husband's brother refused to "raise up to his brother a name in Israel, he will not perform the duty" of having sex with her. Once she had laid her claim against her new husband the reluctant brother-in-law become husband was ordered to appear at the next council. At that meeting he was interogated—and if her charge was proven and the reluctant husband continued in his refusal to impregnate his dead brother's widow, the scorned bride was allowed to divorce him. Her divorce, in such cases, was exceptionally colorful, for it was meant to be a teaching and warning demonstration. The Law reads: *Then shall the dead brother's wife come before her new husband [who is the brother of the dead man] in the presence of the city elders. She shall loosen his sandle and remove it from his foot. She shall spit into his face and say to him, "This will be done to any man that will not build up his brother's house!" "And his name will be stricken from the dynasty of Israel, and shame will fall upon the family from which he comes.*"[8]

NOTES

1.	Leviticus 20:10; cp. Exodus 20:14.

2.	II Samuel 11:12.

3.	Proverbs 6:26, 30:20.

4.	Numbers 5:12-33 (my translation).

5.	I Samuel 25:2-42; Jeremiah 2:2; cp. Genesis 2:24-25, 3:8, 17, and 4:1, 17.

6.	Numbers 12.

7.	Deuteronomy 24:1f.

8.	Deuteronomy 25:5-9.

CHAPTER EIGHT

THE RIGHTS OF WOMEN

Women in ancient Israel had indirect privileges and rights. Paramount among these indirect privileges and rights were exemptions from adherence and obedience to the commandments which have no set time. This is especially true in the case of finding lost articles. [1]

If a woman should find an object that someone else had lost, she was under no obligation to return it immediately—nor at any specific time. The only obligation required of the woman was to return the found object to its rightful owner before she died. If the person who had lost the object had died in the meantime, the finder was still obligated to return the missing object—and provided that the lost item was returned to the heir or estate of the original owner before the death of the finder the return was considered valid.

If the finder should die before the lost item was returned it was the obligation of her kindred to return it to the original owner. If the return was not made the finder was in divine peril—not however in the sense that she would suffer in a purgatory or hell, for neither state was precisely defined until after the days of the Maccabees, but the divine wrath would be visited "even to the fourth and fifth generation." To avert such familial catastrophy, the kindred made efforts to return the item found by the deceased. Only if all efforts had been expended and the original owner and his/her heirs could not be located was there an opportunity for the finder and her heirs to keep possession of the good.

A second right enjoyed by women in ancient Israel was the right of experiencing childbirth. This "right"—although technically a punishment for consuming the forbidden fruit in *Gan Eden*—was a "privilege" to many women who saw it as a testimony to their being a woman and to the entire psychology of "womanliness".

Giving birth to a child proved, moreover, to her society that she was behaving "modestly and within the limits of God": that she was fulfilling her "marriage obligation" by having sex with her husband at his demand—and that the sex experienced was "just"—that it was sex leading to procreation, rather than mere lust fulfillment.

Childbirth was also a promise of security. For once ancient Israelite woman gave birth to the child, provided that the child lived, the woman could expect honor and respect (although never love, for love was to be freely—and rarely—given), and some security in her old age.[2]

Corelated with the promise of security in her old age, the Israelite woman could count on security and support in her bearing years from her husband—provided that she prove to him continuously that she was a loyal and productive wife. She had the right to expect and to receive financial support from her husband, to anticipate and know a full larder from which she would take flour, yeast, and oils to make bread to knead and fashion into bread she would bake for him in testimony of her fidelity and domesticity. Provided that she did not burn his bread she could count on the home life to be basically peaceful and comfortable, and if her culinary arts increased to a noteworthy excellence she might win from him the favor of new furnishings and even a trinket of jewelry or article of clothing.[3]

Once her living was secured she could expect to have her medical needs met as well. Not only was her husband to provide attention and care when she was ill—especially in childbirth—but also when she was terminally ill: comforting her with promises of internment in family plots or mausoleums, and with remembrances after her passing. At the time of her death she rested secure at peace knowing that her passing will be honored and remembered by her children.[4]

Sexually she also had some freedoms and certain rights provided that any sexual activity did not take place during times of war—when she was considered to be a "spoil of war" in which case her rights ended—or in acts of adultery or "perversion" which was any act that could not lead to procreation within the bonds of matrimony.[5] If she was raped outside of the times of war the father could be compelled to marry her and provide security and livelihood for her, provided that she was not already promised to another man. If she was engaged the law prescribed death for her rapist: *If in the open country a man meets a young woman who is engaged, and the man seizes her and rapes her, then only the man who raped her shall die. But as to the young woman do nothing against her for the young woman gave no offense which is punishable by death—for this case is like that of a man attacking and murdering his neighbor; because he came upon her in the open country, and though the engaged young woman cried out for help, there was no one to rescue her.*[6]

A far more different fate awaited the young woman who was not engaged and was raped. *If a man meets a young woman who is not engaged, and seizes her and rapes her, and they are discovered, then the man who raped her shall give to the father of the young woman fifty shekels of silver, and she shall become his wife because he has violated her...* But even in this strange situation there was some limited justice accorded the victim in line with security, for the law continued: *...he may not put her away as long as he should live.*[7]

The short of these statements is clear at first reading. The rape of an engaged woman was considered equal to adultery: murder or the taking of property, and thus subject to the death penalty. The rape of an woman who was not engaged helped expiate her marriage eventhough the husband had forfeited his right to a divorce by means of the way he secured the marriage. The men who made the laws controled the world, and this avenue to acquiring what they desired was frequently taken, as testified in the cases of Shechem, son of Hamor the Hivite, who seized and raped Dinah, the daughter of Leah. Although the account in Genesis 34 semi-excuses the attack with the qualifier *"and his soul was drawn to Dinah the daughter of Jacob; he loved her and spoke tenderly to her,"* this "love" came only after the attack. The extent of 'the attack is made even more visible with the following text which cites that *"the sons of Jacob came in from the field when they heard of it; the men were indignant, and very angry,"* and determined on vengance. Shechem and his father attempted to stop intertribal warfare over the rape by offering to intermarry their people with Jacob's—but the Jacobites were unwilling because the men of Hamor's tribe were uncircumcised. The extent of the war and its costliness probably was more important than the desire of Shechem for Dinah, for the two men had to argue with their kindred to undergo the painful operation. Yet in the end they were successful and they were circumcised.

Jacob and his sons suddenly go back upon their word. Eventhough Shechem and Homar and their male kindred and tribalmen underwent the circumcision to fulfill the request of Jacob and his men, *"on the third day, when they were sore"* from the circumcision, in true Machiavellian manner Jacob's sons invaded the city of Shechem and Homar and slew both men and their male kindred, and took Dinah home under the excuse *"because their sister had been defiled."* The reason for the attack on the city of Homar may also have been spurred on because of th city's great wealth, for not only did the sons of Jacob avenge their family's "honor"—but enriched themselves as well: taking everything possible, from flocks, herds, children, wives, and all other fashions of wealth. The taking of the wives was certainly by force and rape most assuredly was a part of it since women in this age could expect to be raped during warfare—which was excused by the Law—eventhough the war was technically generated by an initial rape!

Other Biblical accounts of rape must be scrutinized. Not all were condemned because of the force of violence mitted against the woman. Sometimes the rape occurred because the men sought sexual release in any manner—and the woman was the closest available source of "release". This was certainly the case with the men of Gibeah of the tribe of Benjamin who were certainly homosexual, and at the time, sexually excited: *"...the men of the city, certain sons of Belial, came to the house and beat upon the door, crying out to the aged master of the house, saying "Bring out the young man that is visiting you so that we may have sex with him." The head of the house went out to the men and said, "No, citizens, don't do such an evil thing; the man has come to visit me—don't act foolishly. Instead of him I will give to you my daughter and his mistress. I will bring them to you; you can do with them whatever you wish to do—but don't have sex with the young man." But the men would not listen to him—so he went in and forced the mistress out of the house and gave her to them. They had sex with her— raping her all night until morning; when morning came they let her go. The woman rose and returned to the doorway of the house and fell down in the doorway."*

There was little thought given to the suffering of the victim. She was expendable—so that the men could be left alone to visit. Even after her ordeal, she was not taken care of, nor comforted. Instead her "master" commanded her to "Get up, let's get going", forced her onto an ass, and then returned to his home where *"he took a knife, grapped and held his mistress and cut her into twelve sections which he sent to all the areas of Israel, so that all who would view the pieces would take warning...."*[8]

Rape was also the case with the son of David: Amnon, who raped his sister Tamar.[9] In this case it was rape and incest, but the condemnation was spelled out because of the rape—Amnon suffering death for it. His murder was considered a suitable warning for other men who would rape the king's daughter, possibly because Israel wished to divorce herself from any similarity with Egypt and the ruling *pharoah* (or house) of Egypt where incest was the rule and not the exception: for the Egyptians traced their lineage through the female line, and Pharaoh's traced their regnal rights through their mother.[10]

Amnon's case was special since it was not only rape but incest. Israel, like most other ancient Middle East civilizations was opposed to it—but more so than most, for Israel banned sexual relations not only between kin by blood, but also kin by marriage. The reason behind this taboo was the ancient Israeli concept of property: the "nakedness" of a woman belonged only to her husband. To "uncover" it was tantamount to marriage and thus incest was bigamy and adultery: *"None of you shall approach any one who is a close relative to uncover the nakedness, for I am God. You shall not uncover the private parts* [nakedness] *of your father which is the nakedness of your mother, nor shall you uncover her nakedness. You shall not uncover the nakedness of your father's wife, for it belongs to your father. You shall not uncover the nakedness of your sister, the daughter of your father or the daughter of your mother, whether she was born at home or abroad. You shall not uncover the nakedness of your son's daughter or of your daughter's daughter, for their nakedness is your own nakedness. You shall not uncover the nakedness of your father's wife's daughter, begotten by your father, since she is your sister. You shall not uncover the nakedness of your father's sister for she is your father's closest relative. You shall not uncover the nakedness of your mother's sister for she is your mother's closest relative. You shall not uncover the nakedness of your father's brother—that is, you shall not approach his wife for she is your aunt. You shall not uncover the nakedness of your daughter-in-law for she is your son's wife. You shall not uncover the nakedness of your brother's wife for she belongs to your brother. You shall not uncover the nakedness of a woman and of her daughter, and you shall not have sex with her son's daughter or her daughter's daughter for they are close relatives to you, and such would be evil. And you shall not take a woman as a rival wife to her sister, having sex with her while her sister is yet alive."* [11] In short, the Law forbade sexual relations with mother, step-mother, sister or half-sister, daughter, granddaughter, aunt (whether by blood or marriage), nor with a daughter-in-law. Furthermore a man could not marry two sisters while both were still alive—even if he divorced one. The same held true if he sought to marry a woman, and her daughter, and her granddaughter.

In each case the injunctions was aimed at men and against women. It forbade men from having sex with various kindred women, yet it blamed the women if the sex occurred, as is seen in the various punishments prescribed for any infraction of the Law, since the woman was the property, and by "uncovering her nakedness" the property was invaded, the value decreased, and the aura one of evil: *The man who has sex with his father's wife has taken his father's property; therefore the two shall be put to death.... If a man has sex with his daughter-in-law, they shall both be put to death for they have committed incest.... If a man has sex both with a wife and also with her mother they have acted in an evil manner and they shall therefore be burned alive—both he and they—so that there is no wickedness among you.... If a man has sex with his sister, a daughter of his father or a daughter of his mother—and he sees her nakedness, and she sees his nakedness, it is a shameful thing and they shall be banished from the community;... If a man has sex with his uncle's wife, he has taken the property of his uncle; for their sin they shall die childless. If a man takes his brother's wife sexually, it is impure for he has un-covered his brother's nakedness and they shall be child-less.* "[12] In short: death was the penalty for coitus between son and mother or stepmother, between father-in-law and daughter-in-law, although the manner of death was not spelled out (although one can guess at it being by stoning); burning was required when a man was found guilty of hav-ing sex with two women who were mother and daughter; while the entire community was obligated to watch the final dispatch of an illicit affair between brother and sister or half-sister. Childlessness, which rested with the favor or dis-favor of God was the lot of a nephew having sex with his aunt, or a brother having coitus with his sister-in-law (while the punishment for the aunt and nephew is unclear). [12]

Still there were violations—from peasant to king. Yet Israel survived.

NOTES

1. *Baba Batra* 139b. *Ketubot* 67a.

2. *Ketubot* 29a.

3. *Ketubot* 62b.

4. *Ketubot* 64b, 61b, 51a, 46a.

5. Numbers 31:17.

6. Deuteronomy 22:25ff.

7. Ibid.

8. Judges 19.

9. II Samuel 2:13.

10. See my *Woman in the ancient Near East*, p. 70f.

11. Leviticus 18:6-18.

12. Leviticus 20:11-12.

CHAPTER NINE

ROSH HADESH – THE WOMAN'S HOLIDAY

Israeli woman had but one day she could call her own. Her day was *Rosh Hadesh* – a day which continues today.

Rosh Hadesh was both a holiday and a holy day. Its existence was supported by religion, custom and law. It was based upon the biblical account of creation as well as on the Talmud commentary on "the two luminaries."[1] The commentary is best remembered since it springs from the Creation story:

> [In the beginning the sun and the moon were created in the same manner. They were made the same size. These two bodies were animated, and puzzled over their own uniqueness and development. That they were equal seemed to be out of the scheme of things since all of creation was different. They went to the Creator. The moon, who was more daring than the sun (and is presented in the feminine gender) was quick to speak, and asked the Creator] *"Sovereign of the universe, can two rulers share a single crown?"*
>
> *The Creator answered, "Go, and make yourself smaller."*
>
> *"Sovereign of the universe!" the startled moon lamented, "because I presented a*

proper claim..... must I make myself smaller?"
The Creator, realizing the justice of her plea,
compensated for her diminuation by promising
that the moon would rule by night, and that
Israel would calculate days and years by her, and
that the righteous would be named after her. The
Creator also decreed that a sacrifice was to be
instituted to atone for his sin in making her
smaller. And, finally, that in the future, he
would intensify her light to equal that of the sun.

An obvious parallel to the story of the Creation of humankind, this unique tale offers insight into the actual position of woman in the earliest days. She was aggressive and determined to demonstrate her ability to stand for her just rights. Like Eve the moon took the initiate and confronted the Creator (who is here presented in the masculine gender) for a callous and capricious edict which leveled equality. It was the moon who reminded the Godhead of this injustice, and by her plea (or argument), was able to convince God to reverse his stand—demonstrating her resolve to be stronger than the godhead. Furthermore the moon extracted a promise from the godhead: that in the end she would be triumphant—and on her way to this unique triumph, she was to play a special role in the formation and development of the Jewish society. She would determine time and the calculation of time. The righteous would be named after her.[2]

Another unique facet of this story is its admission that God can make mistakes—by God's own admission as well. Not only can God make a mistake—but also an error in judgment. This, however, does not demean the role of God but makes God even greater for God, unlike humankind, is quick to confess his error and then set out to rectify the injustice. Here is a perfect example for humankind to follow and imitate!

From this story the sages found promise for women— one which would be inevitable—to be the saviors of their people. This promise complimented the promise made to Eve in the garden, and was beautifully fulfilled in the account of Miriam's zeal in secreting Moses, and later in the stand of elect women who equally suffered in the desert after the exodus, but stood fast in the faith of Moses:[3]

> *The women heard about the construction of the Golden Calf and refused to hand over their jewelry to their husbands. Instead they said to them, "You want to construct an idol and mask which is an abomination, and has no power of redemption? We won't listen to you!" And the Holy One, Blessed is he, rewarded them in this world in that they would observe the New Moons more than men [by not working], and in the next world in that they are destined to be renewed like the New Moons.*

which is repeated again:[4]

> *Women were enthusiastic about the Mishkan [sanctuary] and reluctant about the Calf, and were therefore rewarded with the observance of Rosh Hadesh as a minor festival.*

It was a special holiday. Women did not work, nor were the men permitted to require them to work. The Talmud was emphatic, reading:[5] *"It is an acceptable custom for women not to work on the New Moon."*

Since the women did not work during Rosh Hadesh, their time was strictly their own to do as they wished. Many visited. Others took walks. Some visited the graves of their ancestors. But soon it became fashionable for women on Rosh Hadesh to resort to the pasttimes which were more common with men—especially gambling. Many in fact became quite expert at the various games of chances—besting not only their own husbands, but other men as well.[6] This could easily have become a problem, but the men determined that the best solution was to allow the women to play the games of chance—during Rosh Hodesh—and no other time!

With limitations placed upon Rosh Hodesh, the day (which occurs only eleven times a year) soon became ceremonial. The ceremony celebrates the life-giving monthly cycle of women. It incorporates much symbolism, especially the symbols of water, spheres, circles, and monthly purifications, as well as seeds of foods which represent life and life giving properties. Culmination comes with the lighting of candles and the bestowing of charity which are coupled with prayers.

Frequently candles are floated in water in symbolism of the moon floating in the ocean of the sky.

After the ceremony a *mitzvah* takes place—one enjoining the celebrants to eat abundantly. Two *hallots* (or rolls) are used (usually round or crescent shaped). The first course consists of egg soup in symbolic remembrance of the seed being dropped into life sustaining liquid. It is followed by two cooked dishes, and much singing. The songs are in celebration of life—and the exclusive time that is known and enjoyed only by the women.

NOTES

1. *Hullin* 60a.

2. Cp. *Megillah* 22b, and Pirke De-Rabbi Eliezer 45.

3. ...*shehen atidot lehithadesh kemotah...* Ibid..

4. *Mekore Haminhagim* 38. Cf. Numbers 10:10, and 28:11. Ord Zaruah assigns Rosh Hodesh to the woman's monthly menstrual cycle—not to the legend of the sun and moon.

5.   *Taanit* 1:6.

6.   See Arlene Agus, "This month is for you: observing Rosh Hodesh as a woman's holiday," in *The Jewish Woman: New Perspectives*, edited by Elizabeth Koltun (New York: Schocken Books, 1976) pp. 84-93.

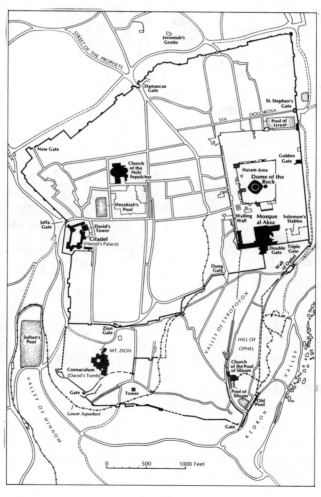

Jerusalem

INDEX

82

83

Select Bibliography

Agus, A.. "This month is for you: observing Rosh Hodesh as a woman's holiday," in *The Jewish Woman: A New Perspective*, edited by E. Koltun (New York, 1976).

Bailey, J. A. "Initiation and the Primal Woman in Gilgamesh and Genesis 2-3," in *Journal of Biblical Literature* (June, 1970).

Ide, A. F. *Woman in Biblical Israel* (Mesquite, 1980).

Ide, A. F. *Woman in the ancient Near East* (Mesquite, 1981).

Ide, A. F. *Woman, Sex, and Religion* (in press).

Kahler, E. *Die Frau in den paulinischen Briefen* (Zurich, 1960).

Koltum, E. *The Jewish Woman: A New Perspective* (New York, 1976).

Muilenburg, J. "Isaiah 40-60" in the *Interpreter's Bible* (New York, 1956) vol. 5.

Noth, M. *The Laws in the Pentateuch & Other Studies* (Philadelphia, 1966).

Westermarch, E. *Early Beliefs and Their Social Influence* (London, 1908).

ABOUT THE AUTHOR

Arthur Frederick Ide was born in Waverly, Iowa. He attended Iowa public schools, and completed his first two degrees in Iowa at State College of Iowa (B.A.), and University of Northern Iowa (M.A.). Additional graduate education was completed at the universities of Cincinnati, Illinois at Urbana-Champagne, Arizona State, and, earning the terminal degree, at Carnegie-Mellon.

Dr. Ide has taught at the Iowa Lakes Community College, Mauna Olu College of Hawaii, University of San Diego, and is currently at Eastfield College, Dallas.

A member of N.O.W., Prof. Ide is active in human rights, and human dignity political programs. This is his thirty-seventh book on the history of women.